Dedicated to the memory of Isaac Asimov

The publisher would like to thank the following for permission to reproduce copyright material:

Photo and art credits:

How Was the Universe Born?:
Pp. 25, 27 (both), © Julian Baum, 1988; p. 12 (upper), © Sally Bensusen, 1988; pp. 12 (lower), 16 (upper), 18 (upper), photographs courtesy of Julian Baum; p. 13, © Frank Zullo, 1987; p. 14 (upper), AIP Niels Bohr Library; p. 14 (lower), Mary Evans Picture Library; p. 15, © Anglo-Australian Telescope Board, David Malin, 1980; p. 16 (lower), © George East, 1978; pp. 17, 21, 24, 32 (upper), 33 (lower), National Optical Astronomy Observatories; pp. 18–19, 22–23, © Brian Sullivan, 1988; p. 20, Science Photo Library; pp. 28–29, front cover and pp. 14–15, © Paternostro/Schaller, 1988; p. 16 (lower), Jet Propulsion Laboratory; p. 33 (upper), 34–35, © Mark Paternostro, 1988; pp. 142–143, © Larry Ortiz, 1988.

The Earth's Moon:
P. 38, Harvard College Observatory; pp. 39 (both), 44–45 (upper and lower), © Sally Bensusen, 1988; p. 40, © National Geographic, Jean-Leon Huens; p. 41 (upper), © Dennis Milon; pp. 41 (lower), back cover and pp. 46–47 (both), 48 (all), 49 (lower), 50 (all), 51 (upper left, upper right, and lower right), 53 (all), 145 (lower), courtesy of NASA; pp. 42–43 (all upper), 145 (lower), Lick Observatory; pp. 42 (lower), 43 (lower), © Tom Miller 1988; p. 45 (upper and lower right), © George East; p. 49 (upper left and upper right), Oberg Archives; p. 51 (lower left), © Alan Bean 1986; pp. 52, 54–55 (upper), © William K. Hartmann; p. 55 (lower), © Ron Miller; p. 56 courtesy Lunar & Planetary Institute © 1985, Pat Rawlings; p. 57, © Mark Paternostro, 1978; p. 58, © Doug McLeod, 1988; p. 60, © Paul DiMare 1986; p. 61 (both), © David Hardy; p. 144 (both), © Garret Moore, 1987.

Quasars, Pulsars, and Black Holes:
Pp. 64–65 (upper), 68, 69 (lower), 78, 80, 83, 146 (lower), © Mark Paternostro, 1988; endsheets and p. 87, © Mark Paternostro 1983; pp. 65 (lower), 72, 82, 85, National Optical Astronomy Observatories; pp. 66–67, © Sally Bensusen, 1987; p. 69 (upper), European Space Agency; p. 75, © Julian Baum, 1988; pp. 70–71 (upper), © Lynette Cook 1988; pp. 70–71 (lower), courtesy of William Priedhorsky, Los Alamos National Laboratory; pp. 73, 81 (right), Smithsonian Institution; pp. 76–77 (all), 86, National Radio Astronomy Observatory; p. 81 (two at left), courtesy of Halton C. Arp; p. 84, ©. Adolf Schaller 1988; p. 146 (upper), © Michael Carroll 1987.

Is There Life on Other Planets?:
P. 104, © Sally Bensusen, 1988; pp. 90 (upper), 90–91 (lower), 99 (upper), Matthew Groshek/© Gareth Stevens, Inc.; p. 13 (upper), © Dorothy Sigler Norton; p. 92 (upper), photograph courtesy of Dr. Bishun Khare/Cornell University; pp. 92 (lower), 93, © Garret Moore, 1988; p. 94, National Astronomy and Ionosphere Center/Cornell University; p. 95 (upper), © Rick Sternbach; pp. 95 (lower), 105 (large), 110, Jet Propulsion Laboratory; p. 96, photograph courtesy of Lowell Observatory; pp. 96 (upper), 97 (upper), © Lee Battaglia; p. 97 (lower), painting by Don Davis, courtesy of Sky Publishing Corporation; p. 98 (upper), The Museum of Modern Art Film Stills Archive; p. 98 (lower), Photofest; p. 99 (lower), © Alan Gutierrez; pp. 100–101 (lower), National Space Science Data Center; p. 101 (upper left), © Michael Carroll, 1988; p. 101 (upper right), Field Museum of Natural History, #B83024c; pp. 102–103, artwork by Kate Kriege/© Gareth Stevens, Inc.; p. 105 (inset), © Dudley Foster, Woods Hole Oceanographic Institution; pp. 106–107 (all), ©Julian Baum, 1988; p. 108, photograph courtesy of NASA; p. 109 (both), © Imre Friedmann/copyright 1982 by the American Association for the Advancement of Science; front cover and p. 111 (both), © Doug McLeod, 1988; p. 113, © George Peirson, 1988; pp. 148–149 (house), artwork by Laurie Shock/© Gareth Stevens, Inc.; p. 148 (top), © J. Coggins 1988; p. 148 (left center), © Theresa Fassel 1988; p. 148 (bottom), © Marilyn Schaller, 1988; p. 149 (top left and bottom), © Runk/Schoenberger from Grant Heilman; p. 149 (upper right), © Betsy Esselman; p. 149 (upper center right), Science Photo Library; p. 149 (lower center right), © Marilyn Schaller.

Did Comets Kill the Dinosaurs?:
Pp. 122–123, front cover and p. 125 (series of 4), 128–129, © Julian Baum; pp. 116–117, 150–151, by Rudolf Zallinger, Peabody Museum of Natural History; p. 118, © Diane Gabriel, Milwaukee Public Museum; p. 119, Terry Huseby, © Discover Magazine (March, 1986); p. 120, © Allan E. Morton; p. 121 (both), Geroge Gerster, Science Source; pp. 124–125, 126, 130–131, 132–133, © Mark Paternostro; p. 127, Leonid Kulik, courtesy of Smithsonian Institution; pp. 134–135, courtesy of European Southern Observatory; pp. 136–137, © Michael Carroll; pp. 138–139 (all), courtesy of NASA.

Isaac Asimov's GREAT SPACE MYSTERIES

Modern Publishing
A Division of Unisystems, Inc.
New York, New York 10022
Printed in Italy

Contents

Introduction

Nowadays, we have seen planets up close, all the way to distant Uranus. We have mapped Venus through its clouds. We have seen dead volcanoes on Mars and live ones on Io, one of Jupiter's moons. We have put spacecraft with measuring devices on the surfaces of Mars and Venus. Human beings have even walked on the moon.

We have detected strange objects no one knew anything about until recently: quasars, pulsars, black holes. We have learned amazing facts about how the Universe was born and have some ideas about how it may die. Nothing can be more astonishing and more interesting.

So let's learn a bit more about the amazing story of our Universe!

Isaac Asimov

The greatest drama of all is to try to understand the Universe as a whole. We can only begin to try to grasp its vastness and to study all the strange things we find in it. Some of these things—quasars, pulsars, and black holes—we didn't even dream of until the last few decades. *Isaac Asimov*

How Was the Universe Born?

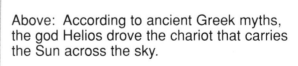

Above: According to ancient Greek myths, the god Helios drove the chariot that carries the Sun across the sky.

Left: Nut, a sky goddess of ancient Egypt.

Right: The stars of summer gleam like jewels on the dome of the night sky.

Primitive Ideas

Long ago, human beings could only suppose that the Universe was what it looked like to them.

The Earth? It seemed to be no more than a round patch of flat ground, not very big. The sky? It seemed to be a solid dome that came down to meet the ground all around, at places not far off. The Sun? It traveled across the sky to give us light and warmth. The sky was blue when the Sun was present, but turned black when it set. In the night sky, there were many, many specks of light — stars — in the dome of the sky. The Moon, which went through a change of shape every month, moved among the stars. A few stars were brighter than the others, and they also moved.

Where Is Earth?

The ancient Greeks said that Earth was a large sphere and thought it was at the center of the Universe. They thought that the Moon circled around the Earth. Outside the Moon's orbit circled Mercury, Venus, the Sun, Mars, Jupiter, and Saturn. Outside the orbits of all these bodies were the sky and the stars.

In 1543, Copernicus (pronounced co-PER-nic-us) showed that it made more sense to suppose that the Sun was at the center, and that all the planets moved around it. Earth was one of the planets, and it went around the Sun, too. Beyond that were the stars, but they weren't attached to the sky. Later, Edmund Halley found out that the stars moved, too.

Did the death of a star cause the birth of _our_ star?

The Solar system formed from a gigantic cloud of dust and gas a little less than five billion years ago. That cloud of dust and gas must have existed all through the life of the Universe. So it was perhaps 10 to 15 billion years old when it began to collapse to form the Sun and planets. Why did it suddenly start to collapse after all that time? Astronomers think that the shock of a nearby exploding star called a supernova might have started the cloud's collapse. But they still aren't _sure_ that that's what happened.

Left: Nicolaus Copernicus — the Polish philosopher, doctor, and astronomer who showed that the planets circle the Sun.

Lower left: the Copernican system. The Sun lies in the center and Earth circles around it.

Below: Star trails in a time-exposure photo of the night sky. From where we stand on Earth, the Sun, Moon, planets, and stars all seem to wheel across the sky — small wonder people once thought Earth was the center of the Universe!

Island Universes

In 1785, William Herschel (HER-shell) showed that all the stars formed a large collection shaped like a lens. We call this collection the Milky Way Galaxy. This is our Galaxy, and it is 100,000 light-years across. Each light-year is almost six trillion miles (9.5 trillion km) long.

There are other galaxies as well. They look like cloudy patches in the sky, but they are really other galaxies very far away. The closest large galaxy is the Andromeda Galaxy, which is over two million light-years away. Many other galaxies are scattered through space. There might be a hundred billion in all!

The German-born English astronomer William Herschel, discoverer of the planet Uranus. He designed the best telescopes of his time.

If we could view our Milky Way from the outside, it would look like the Great Galaxy in Andromeda, seen here without the aid of a telescope.

Right: Through a telescope, ragged dust clouds appear around the Andromeda Galaxy's core. Over two million light-years away, it's the closest galaxy that resembles our own spiral, the Milky Way. (The white streak across the sky is the light reflected off an artificial satellite moving overhead.)

The Red Shift

In 1842, Christian Doppler explained why anything noisy sounds more shrill when it comes toward you, and sounds deeper when it goes away from you. A similar kind of change, or shift, happens with light.

Austrian scientist Christian Doppler.

Every star sends out light waves. The light appears bluer if the star is coming toward us, and redder if it is moving away. In the 1920s, astronomers found that most galaxies show a "red shift." This means that they are moving away from our Galaxy. The farther away they are, the faster they move away from us. The farthest galaxies are moving away at thousands of miles a second!

When light from a star or galaxy is spread out into a rainbow of color, dark lines show up where light has been absorbed by the atoms of that star or galaxy. The lines in the light of distant galaxies are shifted toward ever redder light as we look farther away.

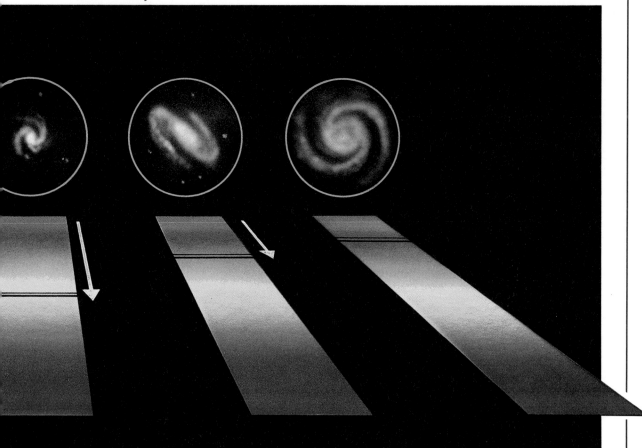

19

The Outer Limits

The most distant galaxies we can see are hundreds of millions of light-years away. In the 1950s, astronomers discovered certain galaxies that sent out radio waves. These galaxies were studied carefully, and the light waves they sent out looked very strange. In 1963, astronomers found that this was because the light waves were very stretched out.

Galaxies like this are called quasars. Quasars had the largest red shifts known, so they must be very far away. Even the closest quasars are a billion light-years away. One quasar discovered recently is 12 billion light-years away! So when we look at quasars, we are looking back into a time before our Sun was born!

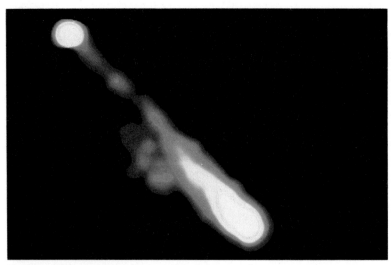

Radio telescopes created this image of a huge gas jet erupting from quasar 3C 273. The jet is a million light-years long!

Right: Appearances can be deceiving. A bridge of gas seems to connect a quasar (top) to a much closer galaxy (below). Astronomers believe that such connections are optical illusions. Colors are added to the picture to bring out faint details.

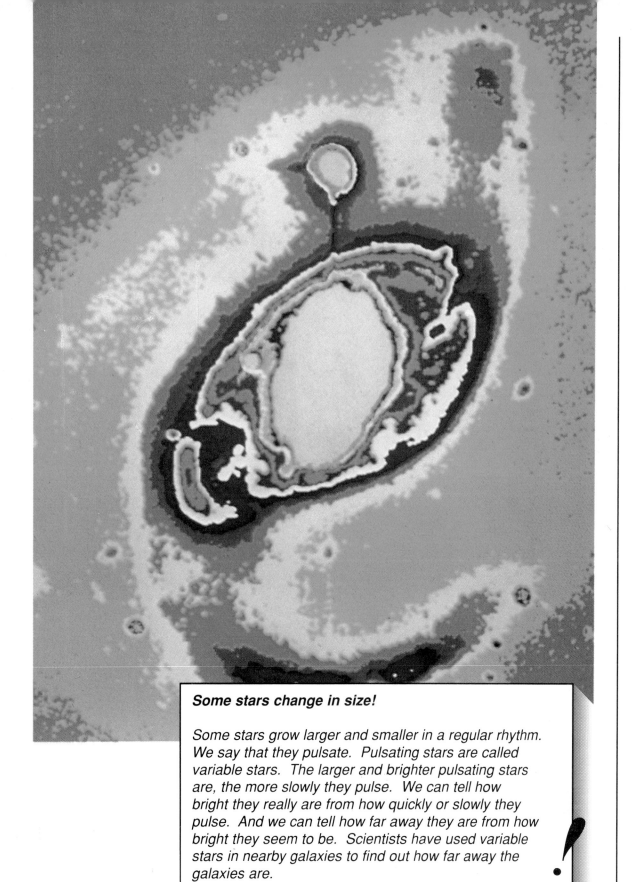

Some stars change in size!

*Some stars grow larger and smaller in a regular rhythm.
We say that they pulsate. Pulsating stars are called
variable stars. The larger and brighter pulsating stars
are, the more slowly they pulse. We can tell how
bright they really are from how quickly or slowly they
pulse. And we can tell how far away they are from how
bright they seem to be. Scientists have used variable
stars in nearby galaxies to find out how far away the
galaxies are.*

The Universe — It's a Big Place!

The known planets orbit the Sun in a region only about seven billion miles (11 billion km) in diameter. That's just a little over a thousandth of a light-year. The nearest star is 4.2 light-years away. That's thousands of times as far away as the farthest planet in our Solar system.

The farthest stars in our Galaxy are 100,000 light-years away. The Andromeda Galaxy is over two million light-years away,

We think of Earth as quite big, but this painting puts us in our place! From left to right, we see that Earth is just one of nine worlds orbiting the Sun. Our Sun itself is just one of 200 billion stars in the Milky Way Galaxy. The Milky Way is but one of many galaxies in our cluster, and one of <u>billions</u> of galaxies in the Universe.

but it's our next-door neighbor. The farthest known quasar is about 12 billion light-years away.

In all the Universe, there are about 100 billion galaxies. And each galaxy contains about 100 billion stars.

Imagine how small our own Earth is in comparison!

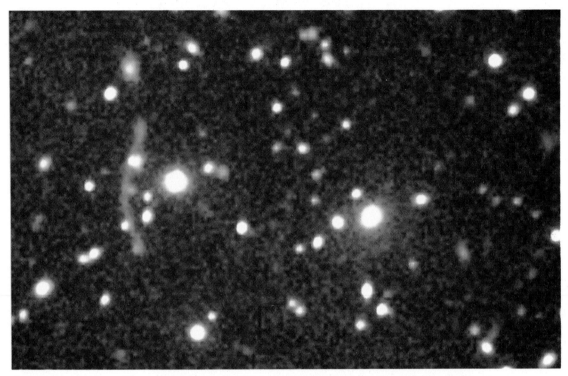

A galaxy cluster. The glowing arcs in this picture might be formed by light pulled off course by a tremendous but unidentified source of gravity. No one knows for sure.

The Expanding Universe

Why are all the galaxies moving away from us? Why should the galaxies farthest away from us move away the fastest? What's so special about us?

The answer is that it isn't us at all! Galaxies exist in groups called clusters. Every cluster moves away from every other cluster. No matter what cluster we might live in, the others would be moving away from us. The Universe is always expanding — growing larger. The space between galaxies is getting bigger. But scientists didn't know this until 1929.

Why is the Universe like soap bubbles?

Throughout the Universe, galaxies seem to form lines and even curves. They enclose large spaces in which there seems to be very little matter. If we could look at the Universe from a great distance and see it all at once, we would think it looked like soap bubbles. Galaxies would be like the soap film making up the bubbles. The bubbles themselves would be empty and come in different sizes. Astronomers still don't know why the galaxies were formed in this way.

"Soap bubble" galaxies.

The Big Bang

The Universe is expanding as time goes on. But suppose we look backward in time.

As we go farther and farther back in time, the galaxies move closer and closer together. If we went back in time far enough, all the galaxies would crunch together into a small space.

That was the way it was in the beginning. The whole thing must have exploded in a "Big Bang." The Universe is still expanding as a result of that Big Bang. If we measure how fast the Universe is expanding and how long it must have taken to reach its present size, we know that the Big Bang happened 15 to 20 billion years ago.

Okay — but what came <u>before</u> the Big Bang?

As scientists try to figure out the history of the Universe, they reach a point where the laws of science don't seem to work. They can only describe the Universe a fraction of a second after the Big Bang. But what existed <u>before</u> the birth of the Universe? One scientist thinks the cosmos might have been born from <u>nothing</u>. But no one can really say!

Imagine that galaxies are like the raisins in raisin bread dough. The raisins start off fairly close together (top). If you could stand on any one of them as the dough expands (bottom), all the other raisins would appear to be moving away from you. As space expands, all the galaxies appear to be moving away from us.

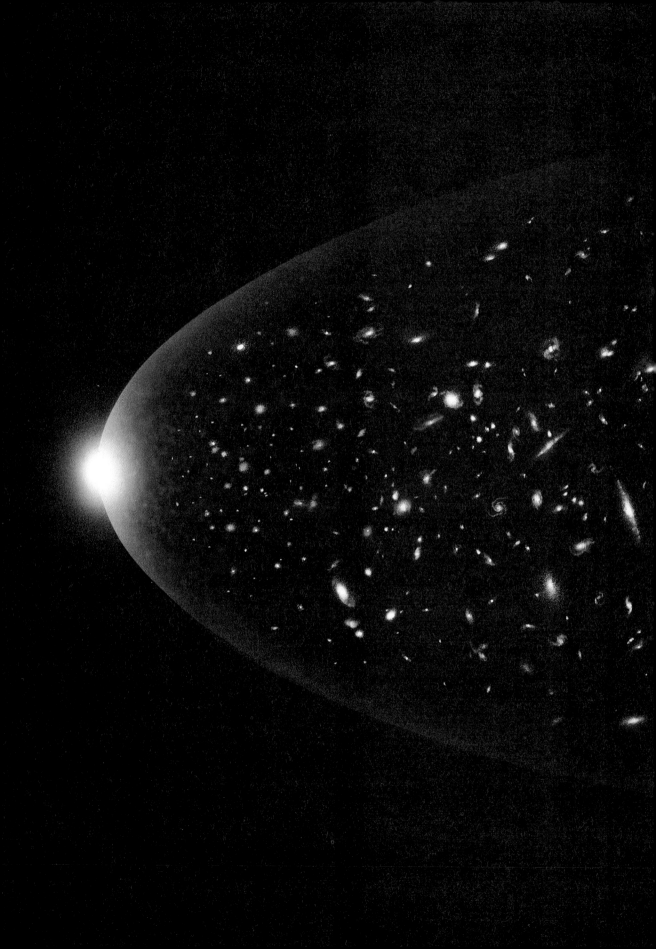

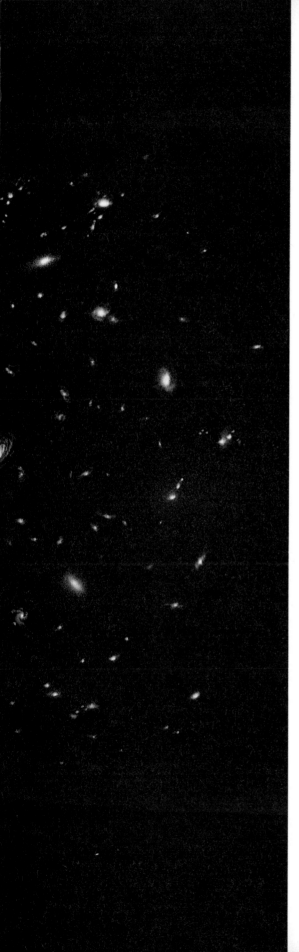

Whispers of the Big Bang

At the time of the Big Bang, all the matter and energy of the Universe was squeezed into one tiny spot! It must have been very hot — trillions of degrees.

But as the Universe expanded, it cooled off. There are still hot spots, like the stars, but overall, the Universe has become much cooler. The light waves of the vast flash of the Big Bang stretched and grew longer as the Universe cooled. Today, they are very long radio waves.

In 1965, those radio waves were detected. Scientists could hear the last faint whisper of the Big Bang of long ago.

This painting shows the history of our expanding Universe. The bright spot on the left represents the Big Bang itself. As you look farther to the right, subatomic particles form, then atoms of matter. Next, gas clumps together to form galaxies. Then, within those galaxies, gas further clumps to make stars and planets.

The Early Universe

Light travels at a speed of 186,000 miles (300,000 km) a second. If a star is 10 light-years from us, its light takes 10 years to reach us.

Since the Andromeda Galaxy is over two million light-years from us, its light takes over two million years to reach us! This means that the farther out in <u>space</u> we look, the farther back in <u>time</u> we see!

Light from the most distant known quasar takes about 12 billion years to reach us. Since the Big Bang happened about 15 to 20 billion years ago, we see distant quasars as they looked when the Universe was quite young. In 1988, astronomers announced that they had found objects 17 billion light-years away. They were galaxies being formed when the Universe was still younger. We can't see much farther than that!

How far is far? The light from our Sun (shown to the upper right of Earth), takes just eight minutes to reach us. Light from the nearest star, Alpha Centauri (the bluish speck shown below Earth), takes 4.2 years. The light we see from the Great Galaxy in Andromeda (the spiral shown lower left) left 2.3 million years ago. And light from the farthest known quasars (upper left) set out 12-15 billion years ago.

How the Universe Changes

Stars stay hot because of nuclear changes in their centers. As a star center grows hotter, the star expands. Eventually, the star explodes and collapses.

When a very large star explodes, it becomes a supernova. Supernovas spread their material through space. In the Big Bang, only the simplest atoms, hydrogen and helium, were formed, but supernovas spread more complex atoms outward.

Our Sun formed from a cloud with these more complex atoms. Almost all the atoms of Earth — and in ourselves — were formed in stars that exploded as supernovas long ago.

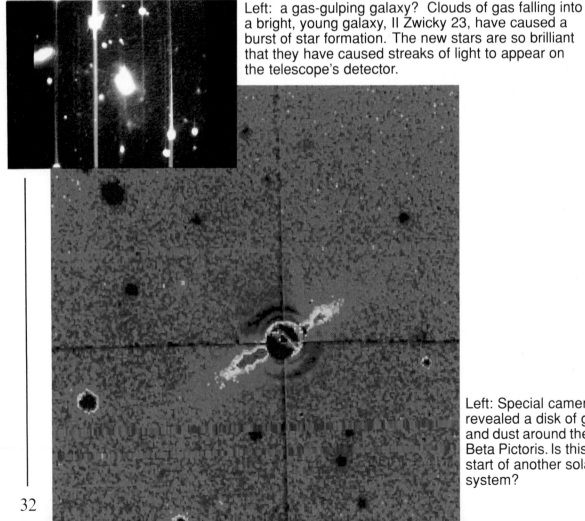

Left: a gas-gulping galaxy? Clouds of gas falling into a bright, young galaxy, II Zwicky 23, have caused a burst of star formation. The new stars are so brilliant that they have caused streaks of light to appear on the telescope's detector.

Left: Special cameras revealed a disk of gas and dust around the star Beta Pictoris. Is this the start of another solar system?

Above: Stars can explode with incredible violence, becoming so bright that they outshine a whole galaxy of normal stars. Supernovas also spread complex elements into space, and the force of the explosions helps stars begin to form.

Left: Galaxy NGC 5128 before (top) and after (bottom) it had a supernova.

A crab in the sky!

In 1054, a supernova only about 5,000 light-years away appeared in the sky. It was brighter than the planet Venus, but a year or so later, it faded away. But what is left of it can still be seen as a small, oddly shaped cloudy patch right where the supernova was. It is a cloud of debris left by the explosion. It's called the Crab Nebula because of its shape. The Crab Nebula has been expanding for almost 1,000 years after the explosion. In its center, there is a tiny neutron star, all that is left of the original giant star that exploded. ●

What Will Happen to the Universe?

When a supernova explodes, what is left of it can collapse into a tiny object with gravity so strong that everything falls in, but nothing comes out. This object is called a black hole. There might be a black hole in the center of every galaxy.

The Universe may expand forever, or its own gravity might some day slow its expansion, and even stop it. It might then fall back together in a Big Crunch. And maybe a new Universe will form in a new Big Bang.

Maybe there was a Big Crunch, or even many Big Crunches, before the Big Bang that formed our Universe. We don't know if there ever was. We're still trying to understand the Big Bang that created the present Universe. That's a big enough puzzle for now!

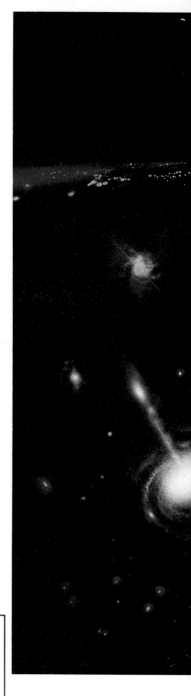

Mini-stars with maxi-mass

When a star explodes and collapses, it becomes incredibly smaller than you might ever expect. It's like breaking up Ping-Pong balls and packing their pieces. Some stars collapse into white dwarf stars. White dwarfs can be smaller than Earth, but they can hold the same amount of matter as the Sun! Even smaller stars, called neutron stars, are formed when very large stars collapse. Neutron stars can be as massive as our Sun, but they might be only a few miles in diameter!

Someday in the very distant future, perhaps the Universe will stop expanding and begin contracting. Everything in the cosmos would fall into an enormous black hole (top of painting) — and perhaps create another Big Bang!

The nearest object of all to Earth is our Moon. It is only about a quarter of a million miles (400,000 km) away. The next nearest object, the planet Venus, is about 100 times as far away. Mars is about 200 times as far away. Everything else is much, much farther. In fact, the Moon is only three days away by rocket ship, and it is the only world other than Earth that human beings have stood on.

Isaac Asimov

The Earth's Moon

A daguerreotype (an early form of photograph) of the Moon made on February 26, 1852. This is one of the first pictures taken of the Moon.

Earth's Neighbor

There is no doubt about it: The Moon is the ruler of our night sky. Everything else in the night sky is just a point of light. But the Moon is large enough and close enough to give us light at night. It is close enough for its gravitational pull to drag the sea upward and cause the tides. We can see both shadows and bright spots on the Moon's surface. These shadows and bright spots have played games with our eyes for thousands of years. Primitive people thought the shadows might be a person. That's why we've all heard about "the man in the Moon," even though we know there's no such thing. Until not so long ago, some people thought the Moon was a world like Earth. Of course, we now know that this is not true, either. Even in ancient times, there were tales about trips to the Moon. Thanks to our modern science and our old-fashioned curiosity, these tales have come true.

Over the years, people have seen many faces in the Moon's surface. Upper: This is how an artist imagines the Moon when the Sun's light reveals only one-quarter of the surface.
Lower: Can you imagine shadows and light forming this jolly face when the Sun's light falls full on the Moon?

Discovering the Moon

In ancient times, people had to look at the Moon with their eyes only. Then, in 1609, an Italian scientist named Galileo built a telescope to make things look larger and nearer. The first thing he did was use it to look at the Moon. At once he saw it was a world. There were mountain ranges, and there were craters. A few craters had bright streaks coming out all around. The shadows on the Moon turned out to be flat, dark areas, and Galileo thought they might be seas of water. It turned out that they weren't, however. There is no water on the Moon — no air, either.

© National Geographic, Jean-Leon Huens

Galileo Galilei (1564-1642) argues with Church officials over his ideas about the skies. What Galileo saw through his telescope was so different from what people believed that they must have thought there was a problem with his scope!

© Dennis Milon

This is a photograph of the Moon taken in 1960 from Houston, Texas. Although it would not have been quite so clear to Galileo, imagine his pleasure at seeing this surface through his telescope!

The crater Langrenus. To get from one side to the other, you would have to walk about 85 miles (137 km). This is how Langrenus looked on December 24, 1968, from the Apollo 8 spacecraft orbiting the Moon.

NASA

The moon's craters — look out above!

The craters and "seas" on the Moon were caused by meteorites bombarding the Moon's surface. Most of these strikes occurred in the early days of the Moon. But meteor strikes may even have happened in recent times. On June 25, 1178, five monks in Canterbury, England, recorded that "a flaming torch sprang up, spewing out fire, hot coals, and sparks" from the edge of the Moon. We think that a meteorite must have struck the Moon just at the edge of the far side. There's simply no way of predicting when a large object might strike the Moon — or the Earth.

The Moon's Changing Face

Lick Observatory

New (or Crescent) Moon   First Quarter

The phases of the Moon as photographed from Earth.

Is moonlight really light that comes from the Moon? We know that it is not. The truth is, the light we see when we look at the Moon is sunlight that shines on the Moon's surface. The Moon moves around the Earth, and as it does, different parts of it are lit by the Sun. When it is on the opposite side of the Earth from the Sun, the side we see is all lit. We call this view the "full Moon." When it is on the side of the Earth that is near the Sun, the lit side is away from us and we don't see the Moon. In between, the Moon is partly lit. These are the Moon's phases. It goes from full Moon back to full Moon in about a month. In ancient times, people used the Moon as a calendar to tell time.

© Tom Miller 1988

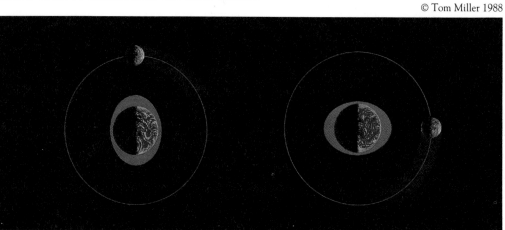

Tides are caused by the pull of the Moon's gravity on the surface of the Earth. Land is too firm to respond noticeably to the pull, but water stretches toward and away from the Moon because of gravity. In this diagram, the light blue egg-shaped area shows how the tides rise and fall around the world as the Moon orbits Earth.

bous Moon   Full Moon   Gibbous Moon   Last Quarter   Old Moon
:ing   Waning

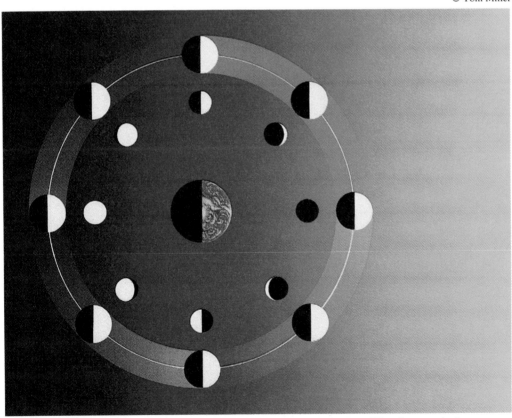

Images of the Moon reflecting sunlight as it circles Earth. The inner circle
shows us what the phases of the Moon look like from Earth as sunlight is
reflected on the Moon's surface. The outer circle shows us what the
Moon might look like from a point in space high above our North Pole.
From there, the Moon doesn't seem to go through phases at all.

Hide-'n'-Go-Seek

© Sally Bensusen 1988

Usually, when the Moon travels about the sky and approaches the Sun's position, it goes a little bit above or below the Sun. Sometimes, though, it cuts right across the Sun and hides it for a while. This is called an eclipse. This was very frightening to ancient people who didn't know what was going on. They thought the Sun was dying! However, an eclipse of the Sun only lasts for a few minutes. On the other hand, sometimes, when the Moon is full and on the <u>opposite</u> side of the Earth from the Sun, it passes through the Earth's shadow. When the Earth's shadow falls on the bright side of the Moon, it makes the inner part of the Moon's surface dark. Then there is an eclipse of the <u>Moon</u>. That can last a couple of hours.

It is okay to watch an eclipse of the Moon, but staring into the Sun can hurt your eyes very badly. So you must never directly watch an eclipse of the Sun. And that means no telescopes or binoculars, either!

During a total eclipse of the Sun, the Moon blocks out the Sun's light from part of Earth. Within the smallest circle in this diagram, the sky would be quite dark and a person's view of the Sun would be that of the total eclipse. People within the outer circle would find daylight to be a strange kind of shadow and the Sun only partly eclipsed by the Moon. The photo above was taken from Earth during an actual eclipse. It gives a spectacular view of the Sun's corona.

During a Lunar eclipse, Earth comes between the Moon and the Sun and casts its shadow on the bright side of the Moon. The diagram illustrates this, and the photo shows it as it is happening. If you happen to be on the night side of Earth during a Lunar eclipse, you will be able to see the effects on the Moon as we slowly slide between Moon and Sun.

The Earth-Moon system. Compared to other natural satellites throughout the Solar system, our Moon is so big that we might ask whether Earth is more the Moon's <u>partner</u> than its <u>parent</u>. This photo was taken from a craft in Lunar orbit. It dramatically shows the blue Earth on the Moon's horizon.

The Double Planet Earth-Moon?

The Moon is quite large. It is 2,160 miles (3,456 km) across, a little over a quarter as wide as the Earth. The Moon's surface is as large as North and South America put together. The Moon isn't the only large satellite in our Solar system. Jupiter has four large satellites, two of them larger than the Moon. Saturn and Neptune each have a satellite larger than our Moon. However, Jupiter, Saturn, and Neptune are giant planets. It is amazing that a planet as small as Earth should have so large a satellite. Considering how small Earth is and how large the Moon is, Earth and Moon together are almost a double planet.

Will the real double planet please stand up?

The Moon has only 1/80 the mass of the Earth. Still, other planets have satellites with only 1/1,000 their own mass, or less. That is why Earth-Moon is considered to be a kind of double planet. But in 1978, it was discovered that the distant planet Pluto had a satellite. Pluto is a small world, even smaller than the Moon. Its satellite, Charon, is smaller still, but it is one-tenth the size of Pluto. Now it's Pluto-Charon that is the nearest thing to a double planet, especially now that astronomers believe Pluto and Charon are so close that they even share the same atmosphere! Earth-Moon is only in second place.

NASA

A composite photo of Earth-Moon as a double planet. Notice how close the Moon and Earth are in size. The view of the Moon is from Apollo 11 as it returned to Earth. The photo of Earth was taken from Apollo 17. You can see the weather systems in the Southern Hemisphere. Can you also make out Africa?

Exploring the Moon

We Earthlings have never been happy just to sit and stare at the Moon. Almost as soon as we began sending rockets into outer space in the 1950s, we aimed them in the direction of the Moon. In 1959, the Soviet Union (now referred to as the Russian Federation) sent a rocket past the Moon. It took pictures of the far side of the Moon, which we never see from the Earth. Later, in that year a Soviet rocket (with no people on board) landed on the Moon. US rockets were soon doing the same thing and were being put in orbit about the Moon. These Lunar Orbiters photographed all parts of the Moon close up. Scientists got to see all the details of the Moon's surface. Soon we would see even more.

The far side of the Moon. The crew of Apollo 13 took these photos as they passed around the Moon. Upper: The large Lunar "sea" is called Mare Moscoviense after Moscow in the Russian Federation. The large crater on the horizon has the hefty name of International Astronomical Union Crater No. 221.

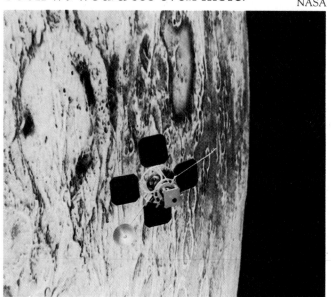

Models show an orbiting spacecraft circling the Moon and taking photographs less than 30 miles (48 km) from the Moon's surface.

Zond-3 probe. This Soviet
spacecraft flew around the
Moon and back to Earth.

Luna 3 probe. This Soviet research
probe skimmed the Moon's surface
to take photographs. In 1959, it
produced the first photos we've
seen of the dark side of the Moon.

Surveyor 6, a US soft-landing
spacecraft. It allowed scientists
to analyze the Moon by gathering
material from the Lunar surface.

49

NASA

NASA

Stepping onto the Moon

Eventually, the Soviet Union and the United States began to put people on rockets. These people were called astronauts in the United States and cosmonauts in the Soviet Union. The US, in particular, decided to place astronauts on the Moon. During the 1960s, rockets flew closer and closer to the Moon. Finally, on July 20, 1969, the big moment arrived. Neil Armstrong set foot on the Moon and became the first human being to walk on another world. After that, five more rocket ships landed on the Moon, ran experiments there, and brought back Moon rocks for scientists to study. These rocks would give us a chance to look at the Moon in a whole new way. For starters, we found out for sure what scientists had suspected — the Moon was a completely dead world.

Top left: That's Astronaut David R. Scott of the Apollo 9 crew working outside his Earth-orbiting spacecraft in 1969. The beautiful blue behind him is Earth. His partners are Russell L. Schweickart and James A. McDivitt.

Top right: Apollo 11 crew, left to right: Neil Armstrong, Michael Collins, Edwin ("Buzz") Aldrin. Collins orbited the Moon in Columbia, the command module, while Armstrong and Aldrin settled into the Moon dust in the Lunar module Eagle on July 20, 1969.

NASA

With no air on the Moon to blow it away, Buzz Aldrin's footprint could remain as it is shown here for billions of years. Of course, we Earthlings may have other plans for this stretch of Lunar real estate!

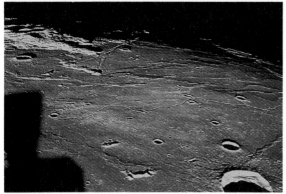

The Apollo 11 crew took this photo (left) of the Moon's surface in 1969. This is actually the approach to Apollo Landing Site 2 in the Sea of Tranquillity.

Alan L. Bean, pilot for Apollo 12, gathers Lunar soil for research in 1969. Also featured in this photo is Charles Conrad, Jr., reflected in Bean's helmet.

Below: Apollo 15 Astronaut Dave Scott showed a worldwide TV audience that Galileo was right: "Gravity pulls all bodies equally, regardless of their weight." To do this, Scott dropped a hammer and a feather and watched as, with no atmosphere to alter their fall, they hit the surface of the Moon at the same time. Astronaut/artist Alan Bean watched on TV, too, and he painted this picture.

© Alan Bean 1986

Right: the US flag, held in a permanent "wave" by its wire frame, adds a dash of color to the Moonscape. Bundled up in his spacesuit, Apollo 15 Astronaut Jim Irwin also poses somewhat stiffly.

Where Did the Moon Come from?

So now we knew more about the Moon than ever before. But scientists still couldn't say for sure why Earth had such a large Moon. One theory went like this: When the Earth was formed, it spun so fast that a large piece of it split off. The trouble is, Earth never spun fast enough for this to happen. Or perhaps the Moon was an independent planet, and it was trapped by Earth's gravitation when it passed too close and was captured. That didn't seem likely, either. Or perhaps when Earth was formed, <u>two</u> worlds were formed. In that case, Earth and Moon should be made up of the same materials. The Moon rocks showed this was not so. The whole thing was a puzzle.

© William K. Hartmann

In this artist's conception, the Moon is shown having formed when it was much closer to the Earth than it is today. Here we also see a ring of leftover debris accompanying the Moon in its orbit around Earth.

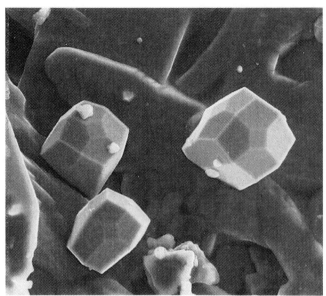

NASA

Some unusual Lunar close-ups.

Upper right: an electron microscope's view of Lunar dust (Apollo 16).

Lower right: Moon rocks (Apollo 11).

Upper left: a farming experiment — soybean sample exposed to Lunar soil (Apollo 15).

NASA

The mystery of our two-faced Moon?

One side of the Moon always faces us. The other side always faces away from us. Once the Soviets and Americans had photographed the other side, scientists discovered that the two sides were quite different. The side that faces us has the large, flat dark areas we call "seas" (even though there is no water in them). The far side has only a few small seas and far more small craters. That would make it appear that meteor strikes and volcanic eruptions — the two main causes of craters — occurred at different rates on each side of the Moon. Why? We're not sure.

A New Theory

Then, just a few years ago, scientists thought about something that may have happened when Earth was first created and other worlds were coming into being. What if one, about a tenth as large as Earth, passed close to our world? It wasn't captured. Instead, it <u>hit</u> the Earth a glancing blow, knocked a piece off, and went on its way. Scientists set up a computer program that showed what would happen if such a world hit the Earth. The computer showed that something like the Moon would be formed out of Earth's outer layers but without the inner ones. That would explain why the Moon doesn't have the same makeup as Earth.

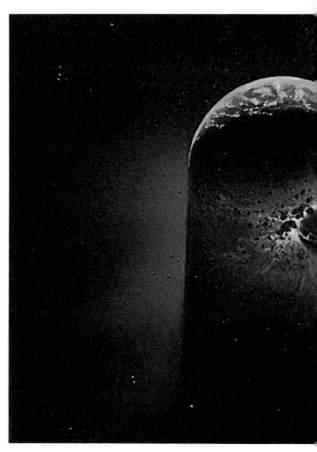

Lunar time vs. Solar time

Ancient peoples who used the Moon for a calendar measured their years in "lunar years." There would be 12 new Moons from one spring to the next. But that wasn't quite enough to fill a whole year. So every couple of years they would add a month and count 13 new Moons to the year. Later, people decided it was easier to make the months a bit longer so that there were always 12 months to a year. The date of Easter is still based on the old lunar calendar. That's why it keeps changing dates from year to year. Muslims also use the lunar months, but with only 12 months a year. That makes their year only 354 days long.

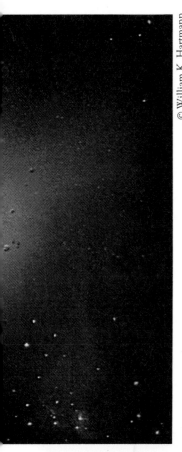

Was it a collision in Earth's formative years that blasted our Moon into orbit? Here are two views. Left: A giant asteroid about one-tenth Earth's size slams into our planet, blasting material out of Earth's outer layer. Below: Another planet collides with ours. After the collision, debris from the other planet spreads out in space and, thanks to its gravitational pull, eventually clumps together.

Our Next Frontier?

Is there any chance that people might one day work — or even live — on the Moon? It wouldn't be easy to try to live on the Moon. It's nothing at all like Earth. For one thing, the surface gravity is only one-sixth that of Earth. Also, there is no air or water on the Moon. And the Moon turns so slowly that the day and night are each two weeks long. During the day, the temperature rises to higher than the boiling point of water. During the night, the temperature gets colder than Antarctica. And without an atmosphere, there is nothing to filter out the radiation in sunlight, or to burn up the little meteorites that are always striking. There is also no magnetic field to turn away cosmic rays.

© LPI 1985, Pat Rawlings

A child and an adult survey the scene of this Lunar base. Here is where the mining of our Moon's natural resources takes place. The six-mile-long (10-km-long) mass driver shown here would provide the boost needed to power payloads off the Moon.

Another artist's conception of a Lunar base — a colony where people live, work, and play as Lunar residents. In both these views of life on the Moon, people must live within the totally artificial environments of their buildings, vehicles, and spacesuits. Such a setting might help prepare future "space people" for their lives as permanent settlers of the cosmos.

A Lunar magnetic field — yes or no?

The Earth has a magnetic field, but the Moon does not. Earth has a large, hot core of liquid iron that swirls as the Earth rotates. That produces the magnetic field. The Moon is less dense than Earth, so it must have only a small core of heavy iron, perhaps none at all. Even if it had a metal core, the Moon isn't large enough to keep it hot and liquid. Still, the Moon's rocks show signs that they were affected by magnetism. Could the Moon in its early days have had a hotter center than now? Could it have had a magnetic field that would have affected its early history? We aren't sure.

Living on the Moon

Does living on the Moon interest you? It sounds as if it could be a tough life. But it might still be possible to live on the Moon, if people stayed a few yards <u>under</u> the surface. There, the temperature is always mild, and people would be protected from the Sun's radiation, from meteorites, and even from cosmic rays. People on the Moon could do valuable work by setting up mining stations. The Moon's surface could yield all the construction metals, as well as oxygen, glass, and concrete. People could make building parts that would be fired into space easily because of the Moon's low gravity. These parts would be used to build places where people could live and work out in space.

The tides — are they wearing Earth down?

Because the tides rise and fall, there is friction of water against the shallow sea-bottoms. The friction consumes some of the energy of the Earth's rotation. As a result, our days are slowly growing longer and the Moon is slowly moving farther away. These changes are so slow that in all history they haven't been noticeable. In very old times, however, the Moon was closer to Earth, the day was shorter, and the tides were higher. How did this affect the development of life? Did the higher tides make it easier for sea life to crawl out on land? We just don't know.

A robot craft operated by a cosmic construction worker puts layers of insulation made from Lunar soil on an immense colony between Earth and the Moon. Other craft approach the docking area, which is the light spot on the colony's "roof," and tube-like structures on the top are what dozens of human workers call home. These details give you an idea of the size of this human habitat in space.

Science from the Moon

Someday, we may mine the Moon for building materials and energy resources. But there are other uses for the Moon, and we must be careful not to disturb the Moon too much. The Moon is smaller than the Earth, and it has changed less since the early days of the Solar system. This means that we can study the first billion years of the Solar system easier on the Moon than on Earth. Then, too, on the far side of the Moon we can set up large light-telescopes and radio-telescopes. There would be no atmosphere to interfere, no Earthly lights or radio signals. We could see farther and more clearly into deep space and learn about the very early days of the Universe.

Who knows what mysteries we may uncover about our Earth—and our Universe—now that we have walked on the Moon?

© Paul DiMare 1986

Imagine what it would be like to look at space from a site on the Moon. In this artist's conception, Russian and US workers break ground for a huge multi-mirror telescope on the far side of the Moon. In the background is a radio/optical observatory.

Imagine seas on a terraformed Moon! By creating an atmosphere on the Moon, we could capture sunlight and turn the Moon into a celestial tourist trap. This would be fun, but many scientists feel it is more important to keep the Moon pretty much as it is. Then we could use it to help us better understand Earth and the cosmos.

Upper: An artificial satellite hovers above the Lunar seas.

Right: Moon tourists have discovered the pleasures of this Moon beach.

We have learned new things about the stars. Fifty years ago, the Universe seemed a quiet place. The stars seemed serene and unchanging. Now we know that stars can explode and leave behind bits of themselves that can do amazing things. These bits are called neutron stars, or pulsars. We know that galaxies can have incredibly active centers, called quasars, and that there can be black holes in space: Everything can fall into them. Nothing can come out! *Isaac Asimov*

Quasars, Pulsars, and Black Holes

The Birth of Stars

The stars do not stay still. And they do not always behave themselves! Some twinkle, and some explode. Some collapse, and some collide with other stars. Some even swallow up light.

With its billions upon billions of stars, it's no wonder our Universe is such a wild place!

To begin with, the Universe was filled with large clouds of dust and gas. Some of these clouds began to contract under their own gravitational pull. In each of these clouds, the matter packed together and became hot. Finally, it became packed enough and hot enough to be a star. Our Sun formed this way nearly five billion years ago.

Stars still form out of clouds of dust and gas that exist today. One such cloud is the Orion Nebula, where astronomers can see small, dark, round spots. These are collapsing clouds that will eventually become shining stars.

The birth of the Sun. Upper left: The birth of the Sun began with the collapse of a cloud of gas and dust. Center: As the cloud contracted, the outer regions flattened into a disk. Right: The center erupted in a blaze — the Sun was born!

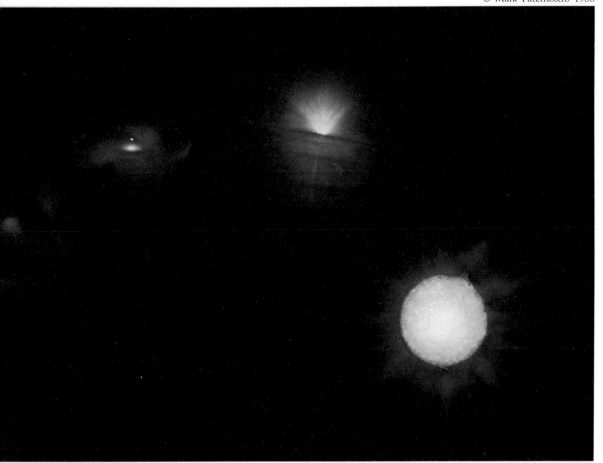

The Orion Nebula: A spectacular cloud of gases surrounds
several hot stars deep inside the nebula. This cloud is
visible to the naked eye as the middle star in the sword of
the constellation Orion. See for yourself some night!

The Life of Stars

Stars come in all sizes. Some are larger and brighter than the Sun; some smaller and dimmer. They are all mostly hydrogen, which is the smallest element. Tiny particles of this hydrogen smash together into larger particles that make up helium, the next biggest element. This collision releases energy that keeps the stars shining. The energy also keeps them from collapsing under their own gravitational pull. Large stars have more hydrogen to begin with, but their centers are hotter than the centers of small stars. So large stars burn their hydrogen more quickly than small stars do.

The creation of helium. The sketch at right shows how the fusion of hydrogen into helium might be performed on Earth to create energy. The two atoms of hydrogen in the form of deuterium (upper left) and tritium (lower left) actually have a bit more mass than the helium (lower right) and neutron (upper right) that are made by this process. The difference in the mass is made up by a huge release of energy. A different form of fusion produces helium in the Sun — and creates sunshine.

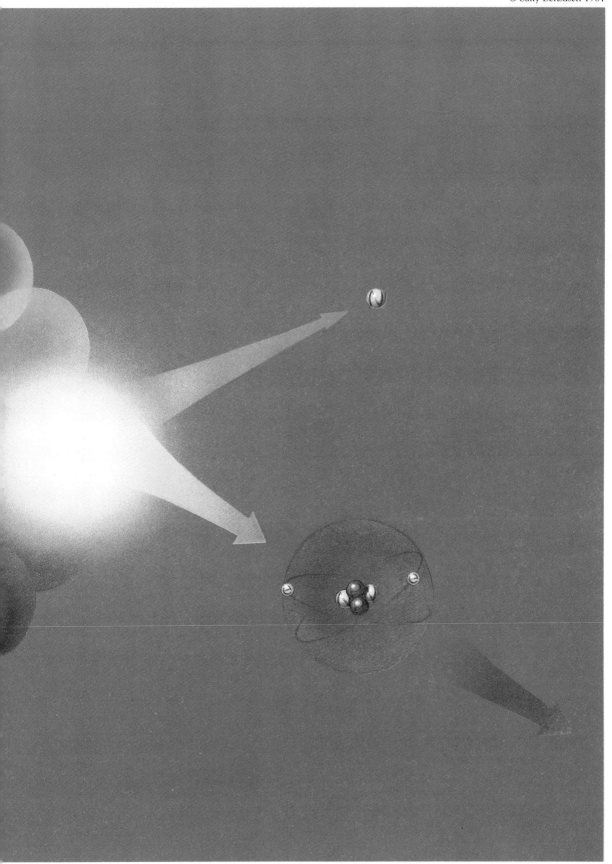

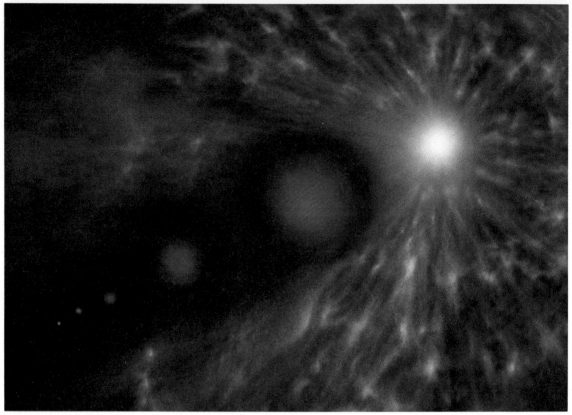

From star to supernova: Going out in style!

© Mark Paternostro 1988

A Star's Violent End — From Red Giant to Supernova

As a star continues to shine, its center grows steadily hotter, and its hydrogen runs low. The extra heat makes it expand. Because of this expansion, the outer layers change to a cool red. The result is a red giant. As the red giant continues to shine, it finally runs out of energy at the center. Then it collapses.

This collapse heats the cool, red, outer layers, and, if the star is a big one, these layers explode. This large, exploding star becomes what is called a supernova. For a while, the explosion makes it shine as brightly in the sky as a whole galaxy ordinarily does.

After such an explosion, matter flies into space or remains behind. The matter that remains behind will become a neutron star or a black hole.

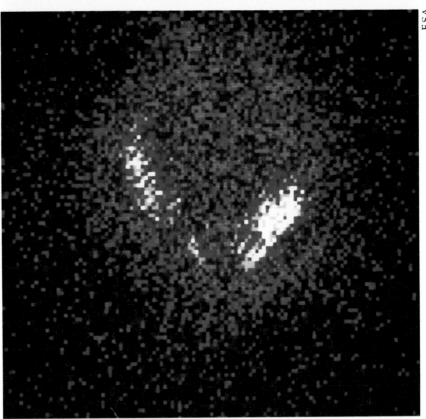

Supernova remnant: This is a satellite's computerized image of material blasted out by an exploding star, or supernova.

Black hole: What remains of a star after it explodes can be so dense that it may imprison even its own light. Though it may be called a hole, it is really an object of great mass. This illustration shows how the immense gravity of the dead star creates a deep "well" from which nothing can escape.

The Big Squeeze
— A White Dwarf

When an ordinary star like the Sun collapses, its gravity squeezes it down to the size of a small planet. All the mass is there, but it has become a small, white-hot body called a white dwarf. If the mass of the Sun were squeezed into an object the size of Earth, or less, a bit of the white-dwarf matter about the size of your little finger would weigh at least 20 tons. If the star is larger than the Sun to begin with, its greater gravity forces it together even more tightly. It becomes a neutron star, with all the mass of an ordinary star squeezed into a little ball perhaps 10 miles (16 km) across!

How much is 20 tons? This picture gives you an idea. It also gives you an idea of what happens when a star collapses into a white dwarf or a neutron star. Imagine a 20-ton cement mixer collapsing into a white dwarf cement mixer the size of your little finger and still weighing 20 tons!

William Priedhorsky

These pictures show a double star system. The larger star (yellow) is a normal star. Its smaller companion is a neutron star. Around the neutron star is an accretion disk. The disk is made up of matter from the normal star that has been sucked away by the neutron star's intense gravity. This matter forms the swirling accretion disk and hits the surface of

© Lynette Cook 1988

A neutron star – small matter, lots of mass!

Our Sun is too small to collapse into a neutron star. But what if a star the size of our Sun could collapse into a neutron star? All its mass would be squeezed into a ball only eight miles (13 km) across. The neutron star would take up only one-quadrillionth of the space the Sun would. But a piece of its matter would weigh a quadrillion (1,000,000,000,000,000) times more than the same size piece of matter from the Sun. Suppose you made a ball-point pen out of neutron star matter. A pen of ordinary matter might weigh half an ounce (14 grams). But a pen of neutron star matter would weigh 15 billion tons.

the neutron star at the center of the disk. The neutron star's gravity is so great that when matter hits the neutron star, energy is released — a lot of energy! For example, a marshmallow dropped on a neutron star would release energy equal to that of the atomic bomb that destroyed Hiroshima!

71

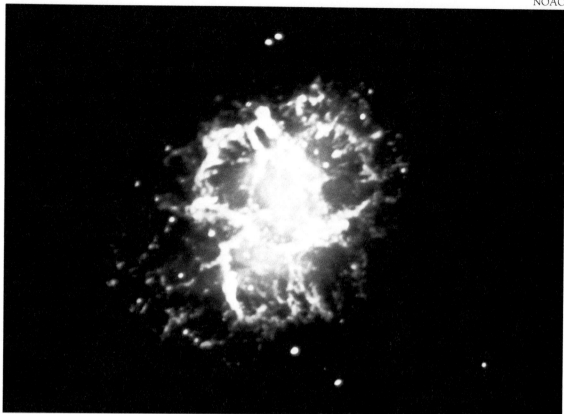

The Crab Nebula: In 1054 astronomers saw a supernova whose "ashes" we see today as a cloud of hot gas. Today's technology can photograph the cloud to reveal its chemical parts. This photo shows hydrogen (red) and sulfur (blue) emissions from the nebula.

Celestial Lighthouses — Neutron Stars, or Pulsars

In 1054, Chinese, Arab, and American Indian sky-watchers looked up to the heavens and saw the result of a supernova that had exploded 6500 light-years away from us. (One light-year is how far light travels in one year.) The supernova formed a huge expanding cloud of dust and gas that we can still see. The cloud is called the Crab Nebula. At the center is a tiny neutron star, all that is left of the exploded star. This neutron star turns 33 times a second, sending a pulse of energy toward us at each turn. This energy is in the form of electric waves called radio waves. We first noticed these pulses in the Crab Nebula in 1969 and began calling neutron stars pulsars. The Crab pulsar sends out pulses of light, too, blinking on and off 33 times a second.

Stars speaking from space!

A young astronomy student, Jocelyn Bell, first detected in 1967 the radio waves that flickered, or twinkled, rapidly from the sky. For a while, some people wondered if they were signals from beings from space. We called them LGM, for Little Green Men. But the twinkles were so regular that we decided they couldn't be of intelligent origin. Ms. Bell had discovered pulsars — spinning neutron stars sending out radio waves with each turn.

Smithsonian Institution

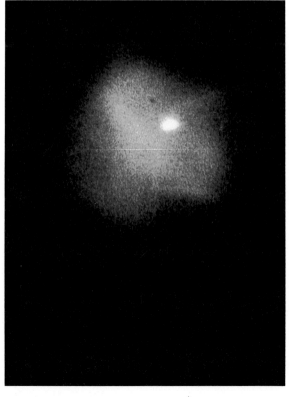

The hot inner regions of the Crab. The bright spot is the Crab pulsar. In one second it blinks on and off 33 times! Here it is with its light on.

A Hole in Space

We know that gravity is a force that makes objects become attracted to one another. But can you imagine what gravity actually looks like? We can picture gravity by pretending space is a rubber sheet. Any heavy object resting on the sheet puts a dent in it. The heavier the object, the deeper the dent. If an object is kept heavy but made smaller, the weight is concentrated on a smaller area, and the dent gets deeper. A white dwarf makes a much deeper dent than the Earth does, and a neutron star makes a still deeper dent. The deeper the dent, the harder it would be to get out of if you fell in. What if something is so small and heavy that it forms a dent too deep for anything to get out of — ever!

Pulsars — you can set your watch by them!

Pulsars turn so steadily that astronomers could use them as nearly perfect clocks. In fact, pulsars have even been used to chart Earth's position in the Galaxy. On board the Pioneer 10 and 11 space probes are plaques that tell about Earth. The locations of pulsars are used as maps on these plaques. Scientists knew that the rates at which these pulsars turned would change very little in the time it might take for these plaques to be discovered in space — perhaps millions of years. So these maps would help extraterrestrial beings find the location of Earth from anywhere in the Galaxy.

This diagram shows the pull of the gravitational fields of several stellar objects: from left to right, the Sun, a neutron star, and a black hole. See how the large Sun barely distorts the grid. The smaller neutron star further distorts the grid with its more concentrated mass. And the smallest object — the black hole — distorts the grid lines most of all with its tremendous gravitational pull.

Black Holes

It is hard to fight the gravity of smaller, more massive objects. A neutron star, for instance, is almost impossible to get away from. Only light, radio waves, and electrons can get away.

And if a massive object were still smaller, <u>nothing</u> could get away from it.

Even light couldn't get away!

If everything fell in and nothing came out, it would be like a hole in space. If even light couldn't come out, we would call it a black hole.

If a large star explodes and its remaining matter becomes small enough and tightly packed enough, it might become a black hole!

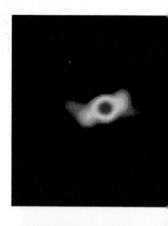
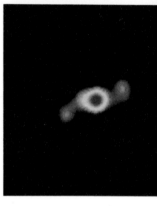

NRAO

Double pulsars — a recipe for trouble?

Astronomers have found cases where two pulsars are close and circling each other. All the while, they are giving off radiation and losing energy. This means they get slightly closer at each turn. Eventually, they will collide. What will happen when two pulsars collide? The mass will double. It might grow so large that additional gravity will cause it to collapse into a black hole. How would the formation of such a black hole appear to our instruments? We just don't know.

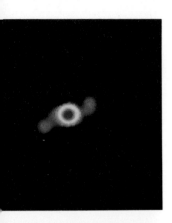

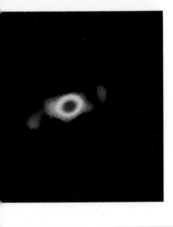

These four pictures, taken by a radio telescope, show a star called SS 433 at one-month intervals. The star is shooting out twin jets of hot gas from its center. The jets are moving away from the star at a speed of 180 million miles (290 million km) per hour — one-quarter the speed of light! Some scientists think that this star may be a black hole.

NRAO

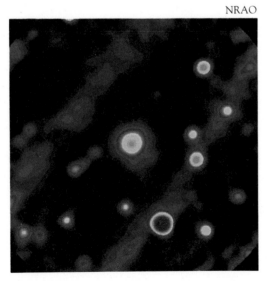

This radio image records a possible black hole in the Andromeda galaxy.

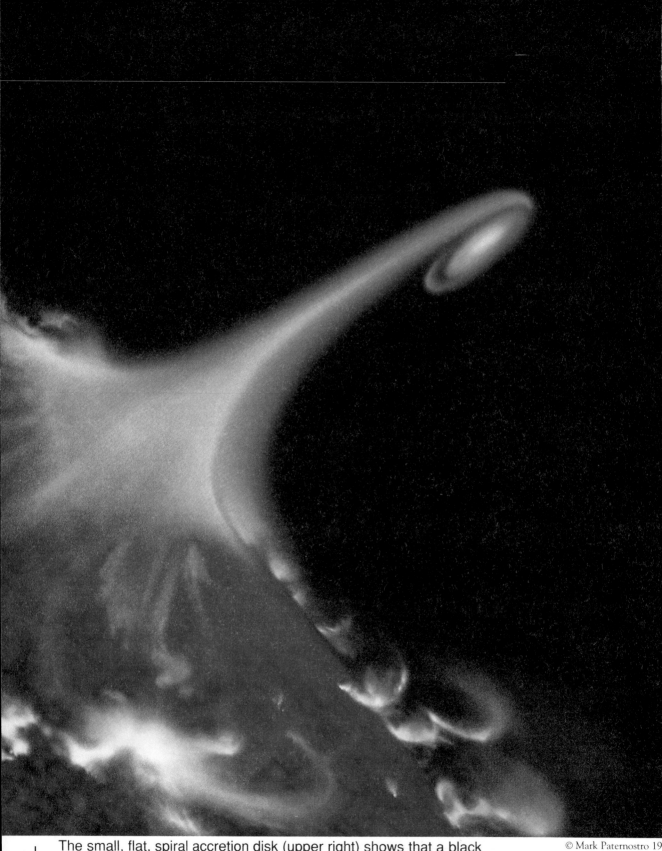

The small, flat, spiral accretion disk (upper right) shows that a black hole is stealing matter from its neighboring star. X-rays given off by the whirling matter tell us we're looking at a black hole. The black hole itself is invisible.

Finding Black Holes

If even light can't get out of a black hole, how can we see it and know it's there? How can we know if black holes exist?

Well, we know because of matter from nearby stars. If the black hole is near some star, it attracts matter from the star. The matter whirls around and around the black hole, creating a flat spiral called an accretion disk. As the matter whirls, it gives off x-rays, loses energy, and finally falls into the black hole. We can't see the black hole, but we can detect the x-rays. In the constellation Cygnus, for example, astronomers have detected x-rays from a large star that seems to be whirling around something we can't see.

That "something" is probably a black hole.

Mini-black holes: a maxi-problem?

A scientist, Stephen Hawking, has shown that black holes can very slowly evaporate and turn into thin gas. The smaller they are, the more quickly they evaporate. When the Universe began, perhaps black holes of all sizes were formed. Some might have been mini-black holes, having about the same mass as planets or even asteroids. If these are scattered through space, we won't be able to detect them unless they are really close. What would happen to us if a mini-black hole approached our Solar system? We don't know. But let's hope it would evaporate before it got here!

© Mark Paternostro 198

Astronomers think this is what the central depths of some galaxies may look like: a black hole at the center both drawing in stellar matter and shooting out jets of excess matter that the black hole cannot absorb quickly enough. These jets shoot out way beyond the galaxy.

What's Going On in There?

We can't see into the central depths of a galaxy. A mass of stars blocks the view. But radiation in the form of radio waves and x-rays comes out of the center, and we can detect that radiation. It takes a lot of energy to form that radiation. Where does it come from? Some astronomers suspect there are black holes at the centers of at least some galaxies. Matter from nearby stars spirals in, producing the radiation. Ordinary black holes, like the one in Cygnus, may only be as massive as large stars. But black holes in the centers of some galaxies may be as massive as a million stars, or even a billion stars! With all that mass squeezed together so tightly, the gravitational pull of these centers must be incredible!

Halton C. Arp   Smithsonian Institution

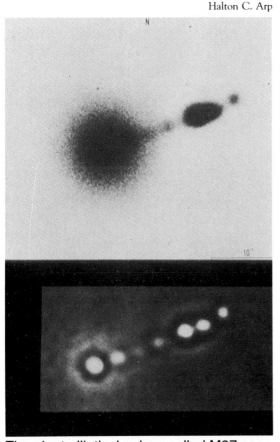

The giant elliptical galaxy called M87 seems to center on a black hole. Billions of stars appear to orbit about a huge object that does not give off light, and scientists think that a black hole center may have consumed the mass of five billion stars the size of our Sun! In these pictures, you can detect the jet projecting from M87's core.

Quasars — Light from the Edge of the Universe?

The Universe never stops coming up with objects to fascinate and puzzle us. One group of objects looked like faint stars. Astronomers once thought these objects were ordinary stars of our own Galaxy — except that they gave off radio waves. But then astronomers watched them closely and studied their light. In 1963, astronomers figured out that these objects were anywhere from one billion to ten billion light-years away. Astronomers soon found many more of these "stars" that were not radio sources but were just as distant. And as recently as 1987, British and American astronomers detected an object that may be 12 billion light-years away. These objects are galaxies so far off that they wouldn't normally be seen except that their centers are unusually bright — a hundred times brighter than ordinary galactic centers. These centers are called quasars.

The word quasar comes from two words, "quasi" and "stellar." Together, these two words mean "star-like." What makes quasars bright may be large black holes at their centers. These black holes would draw in all sorts of glowing stellar matter, from stars to dust.

NOAO

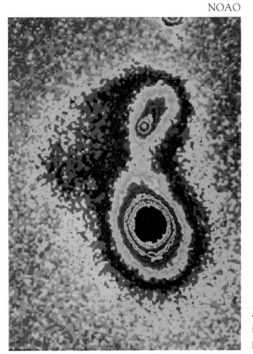

A quasar (top) interacting with a nearby galaxy and drawing in matter to the quasar's center.

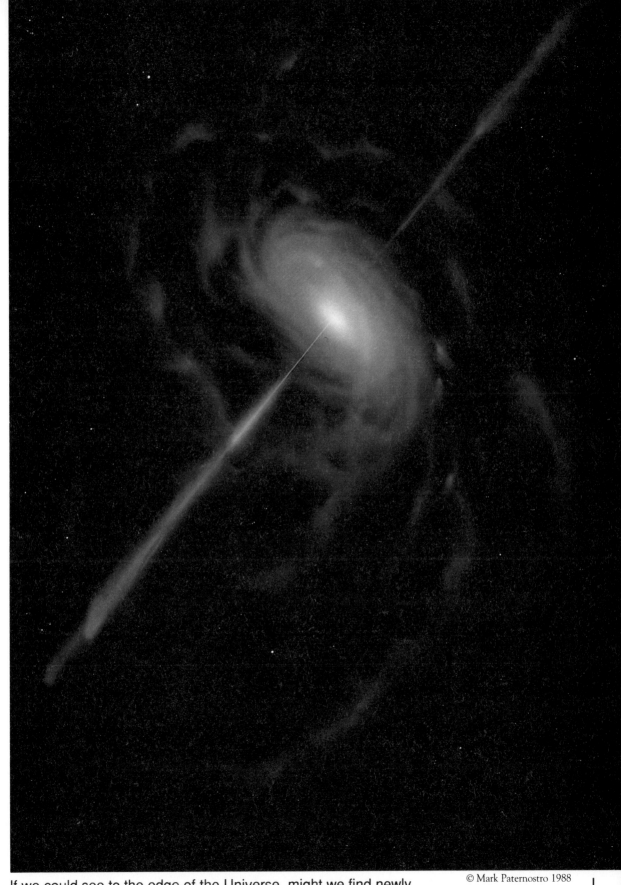

If we could see to the edge of the Universe, might we find newly formed galaxies like this spiral with a quasar as its nucleus?

Seeing Red

How can we tell quasars are so far away? Because certain instruments can spread the light from any star into a rainbow, or a spectrum, of red, orange, yellow, green, blue, indigo, and violet. Across the rainbow are dark lines. When something that gives off light is moving away from us, the dark lines move, or shift, toward the red end of the spectrum. The faster it travels, the farther the shift toward red. Since the Universe is expanding, distant objects are all moving away and show this red shift. The greater the red shift, the farther they are!

The red shift at a glance. A galaxy's hydrogen atoms can emit blue light, as seen in the galaxy at left. However, that same light will appear redder and redder as we look at galaxies located farther from Earth, as shown by the galaxies farther to the right in this picture. The lines on the spectrum below also show a greater shift toward the red end of the spectrum as the galaxies move farther away from Earth.

When quasars were first discovered, they showed a greater red shift than anything else. That is why scientists felt that quasars were the farthest known objects in the Universe. But in 1988, astronomers from the University of Arizona announced that they had detected objects that might even be farther away—and older—then any known quasar. These objects might be as far as 17 billion light-years away! Scientists think they might be primeval galaxies. These would not be quasars. They would be galaxies in their very earliest stages of development.

NOAO

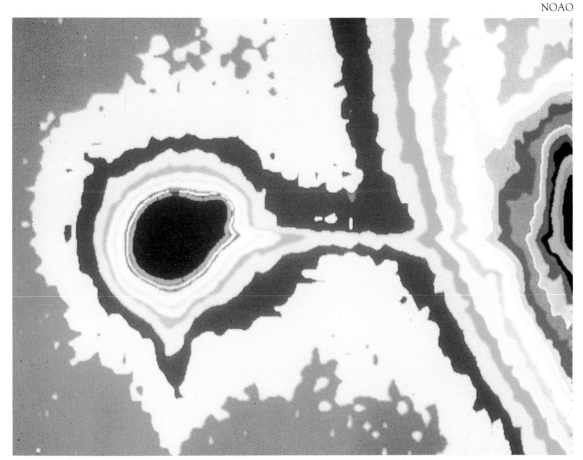

A quasar, left, that seems to be interacting with a galaxy, right. In this computer-enhanced picture, the two together resemble a chicken! The big question: Are the "head" and the "body" actually attached by the "neck" of connecting material? Most astronomers believe the quasar is actually many times farther away than the galaxy.

Was the Milky Way a Quasar?

When we see a quasar 12 billion light-years away, the light from it took 12 billion years to reach us. This means we see the quasar as it was 12 billion years ago. This would be when it — and the Universe, which we think is 15-20 billion years old — were very young. So the fact that quasars are so far away may mean that young galaxies — which shine very brightly — are more likely to be quasars than old ones are. Perhaps our own Milky Way Galaxy was a quasar billions of years ago, but then it settled down. If so, that's a good thing. A galactic center burning away as brightly as a quasar does would fill the galaxy with so much energy that it might be impossible for life to develop in it. And without life in our Galaxy, we would not be here today!

NRAO

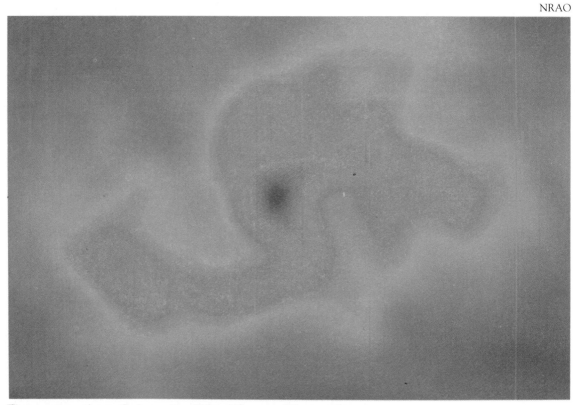

The center of our Galaxy, the Milky Way, emitting radio waves produced by hot gas. In this false-color picture the red shows where the gas is most dense. Could we be just 30,000 light-years away from a black hole?

The Milky Way and Andromeda galaxies: Will they collide? Or will they just slide past each other, sending our Sun spinning off for good? Whatever happens, we've got four billion years to make other plans.

Close encounters of the galactic kind
— a major crack-up in our future?

Our Milky Way and the Andromeda galaxy are moving about in the same cluster. Sometimes we are farther apart, and sometimes we are closer together. Recently a scientist found evidence that the two galaxies will collide in about four billion years. Imagine these two colossal star systems — each containing hundreds of billions of stars — smacking into each other! In fact, though, there is lots of room between the stars in each galaxy and few, if any, stars would actually collide. The galaxies would just slide through each other! But the galaxies would be shaken by gravity, and our own Sun could go spinning off, leaving its home galaxy forever. But don't worry just yet — four billion years is a long time from now!

One thing we have not discovered in the Universe is life. Oh, there is life on Earth, of course, but is that a very miraculous accident so that we are alone in the Universe? Or has life developed on some other world—perhaps on many worlds? That is something that interests scientists very much, and everybody else, too. So in this chapter, we will talk about life on other planets. *Isaac Asimov*

Is There Life on Other Planets?

The Basics — Life on Earth

Over three billion years ago, life appeared on the young Earth in the form of tiny bacteria-like cells. These cells were built up of common types of atoms: carbon, hydrogen, oxygen, nitrogen, and sulfur.

At first, these atoms made up very simple combinations with each other. But sunlight contains energy, and this energy forced the atoms into more complicated combinations, until small cells formed.

On any planet just like Earth, with the same chemicals and temperature, scientists think that life would probably form in the same way. But we don't know how many such planets there might be.

Single-celled bacteria are among the simplest forms of life known. Some bacteria help us digest our food. Some can make you sick. And some, like the bacterium shown above, live in damp sponges and swim across your kitchen table.

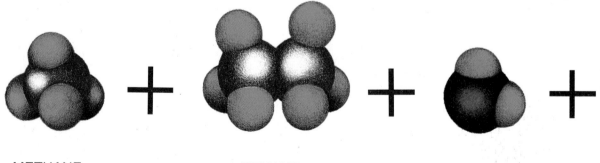

METHANE   ETHANE   WATER

A formula for a "building block" of life. When these chemical ingredients are circulated in water and exposed to energy in the form of sunlight or ultraviolet light, they form glycine, one of the "building blocks" that help form life.

The young Earth's deep basins fill with water, forming our planet's vast oceans. Large meteorites still crash into the surface. These are the conditions under which life developed on Earth!

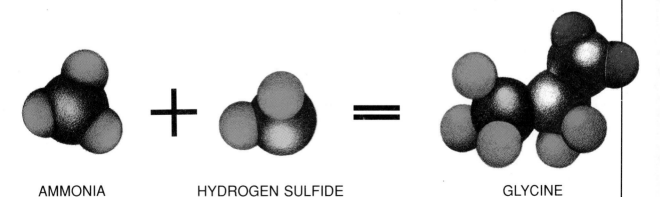

AMMONIA   HYDROGEN SULFIDE   GLYCINE

Above: A spark in a mixture of gases common in Earth's early atmosphere forms a brown tar of complex molecules.

Left: a diagram of a simple life experiment. Experiments first performed in the 1950s showed how simple gases (upper left square of diagram) and electrical sparks (upper right square) could form the complex molecules needed for life on Earth.

Making the Leap — Intelligent Life

For more than a billion years, life on Earth continued to consist of nothing more than simple cells. Gradually, more complicated cells developed, and these cells eventually combined with each other to form larger organisms. The more complicated an organism, the larger its brain and the more intelligent it might be.

It was only a few million years ago that the ancestors of human beings began the process of developing our kind of mind and our kind of thinking. So even though it may be easy for life to develop, it is not so easy for intelligence to develop.

A slice through the history of life on Earth. Important events are noted.

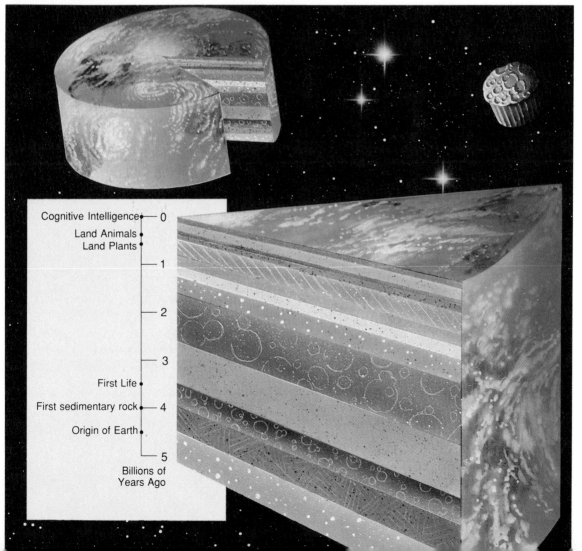

Cognitive Intelligence — 0
Land Animals
Land Plants
— 1
— 2
— 3
First Life
First sedimentary rock — 4
Origin of Earth
— 5
Billions of
Years Ago

Searching the Skies

We now know that the other planets of our Solar system do not have intelligent life. But what if intelligent life forms existed on planets in distant solar systems? How would we discover that such life forms exist? We can't go there, and perhaps they can't come here. Still, they might send out messages in the form of radio waves streaking across space.

It would take time, though. Messages from the nearest star would take 4.3 years to reach us. Messages from the other side of the Galaxy would take about 70,000 years. And of course, we might not understand the messages when we got them. But scientists are trying to detect such messages. Their work is called "Search for Extraterrestrial Intelligence," or "SETI."

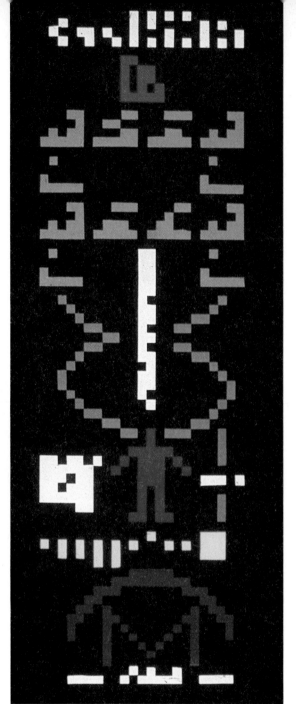

A message from Earth, beamed from a radio telescope in 1974. When properly decoded, it describes our Solar system ( ), the radio telescope that sent the message ( ), and what we look like ( ).

In the distant future, far beyond the cozy confines of our Solar system, dolphinlike life forms make contact with the Voyager probe.

Voyagers 1 and 2 carried a record of music and human voices, and pictures of our planet. The record jacket explains how to play the record and tells where it came from.

Did life's building blocks "invade" Earth from space?

Where did the chemicals needed for life on Earth come from? For years, scientists have thought that energy — from sunlight or even lightning — probably caused atoms and molecules on prehistoric Earth to form these chemicals. Today, scientists have found many of these same chemicals in material from space, like meteoroids and comets. Did life on Earth begin when some of these bodies hit Earth — and brought the basic "building blocks" of life with them?

Wondering and Thinking

For hundreds of years, people have been interested in the possibility of life on other planets. In the 1600s, people discovered that the Moon and planets are worlds, just as Earth is a world. Naturally, everyone wondered if there might be life on those worlds, too.

As late as the 1830s, there were articles in a New York newspaper saying that life had been discovered on the Moon. Many people believed what they read, but the story was a hoax. There is no air or water on the Moon, and so there is no life.

In the 1870s, some astronomers saw straight lines on Mars and thought they were canals built by civilized beings. That was mistaken, too. There is very little air and water on Mars — not enough for complex life forms.

Below, right: Astronomer Percival Lowell made this globe of Mars in 1901. It shows straight lines once thought by some to be canals made by Martians.

Mars — once a living planet?

The Viking probes that landed on Mars found no life there, and all the water on it is frozen. Still, Mars has markings that look exactly like dry riverbeds. Is it possible that Mars was once warmer than it is now and had rivers or even seas? If so, life may have once developed upon it. Even now, there may be simple life forms on it that the probes have not detected. In the future, more probes — or even people — may go to Mars to settle this mystery.

?

96

Left: Believe it or not, this is what some people thought lunar inhabitants looked like!

Below: An artist's concept of what some people thought the Moon looked like. During the Great Moon Hoax of 1835, the New York *Sun* reported the discovery of all kinds of lunar life.

Extraterrestrial Life
in Books and Magazines

In the 1920s and 1930s,
magazines devoted to science
fiction began to appear. Writers
were looking for exciting and dramatic ideas, and they described
our sister planets as filled with life. Usually, the life was described as
monstrous and as threatening to conquer Earth. H. G. Wells had
written a novel about a Martian invasion of Earth as far back as
1898, and many writers followed his example.

These were often very exciting stories, but there was no actual
evidence that such life existed. Though there might well be life
on planets that were like Earth, none of our neighbor planets was
anything like Earth.

Venus — once Earth's twin?

Venus is almost the same size as Earth and is made up of the same kind of rocks. It probably started off like Earth, with water oceans. Over time, however, it became a hot, lifeless wasteland. Venus is closer to the Sun than Earth is, but scientists don't think that is enough to explain the difference. We're not sure what happened to make Venus and Earth so different today. Perhaps if we knew, we could help prevent Earth from one day becoming like Venus.

?

Above: In *War of the Worlds*, H.G. Wells stirred fears of an invasion by terrible beings from Mars.

Opposite: Recognize these characters? Our picture of alien life is limited by our experiences on Earth. For instance, do you think aliens must have two arms and two legs?

Below: Venus might have started off a lot like Earth.

The Space Age — Setting the Record Straight

Until not so long ago, scientists could only study other worlds of the Solar system from a distance. Only from what they saw at these great distances could they reason that these worlds were too cold, too hot, too large, or too small for life to develop. But beginning in the early 1960s, scientists have been sending probes to take pictures of and study the conditions on other planets.

These probes have shown Venus to be boiling hot. They have also shown that Mars has no canals but seems instead to be mostly one large desert. Human beings have landed on the Moon, and probes have landed on Mars and Venus. For now, we have found no signs of even the simplest life, and we are certain there is no civilized life on these worlds.

Below: the surface of Mars as seen from the Viking lander.

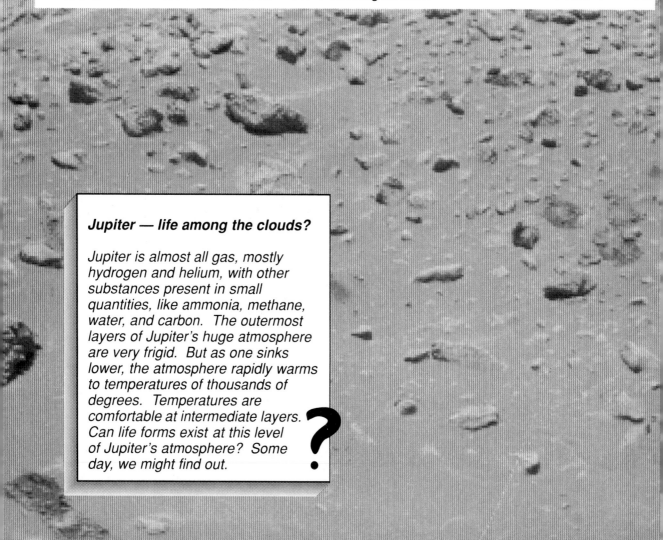

Jupiter — life among the clouds?

Jupiter is almost all gas, mostly hydrogen and helium, with other substances present in small quantities, like ammonia, methane, water, and carbon. The outermost layers of Jupiter's huge atmosphere are very frigid. But as one sinks lower, the atmosphere rapidly warms to temperatures of thousands of degrees. Temperatures are comfortable at intermediate layers. Can life forms exist at this level of Jupiter's atmosphere? Some day, we might find out.

An African plant specially adapted to harsh desert conditions.

An artist's concept of Martian plant life.

Life in the Solar System? — The Facts as We Know Them

We know so much more about the Solar system now than just a few decades ago. We have mapped Venus right through its clouds, and we know that its surface is hot enough to melt lead. It has an atmosphere that is almost 90 times as thick as ours and almost all carbon dioxide. The clouds contain deadly sulfuric acid.

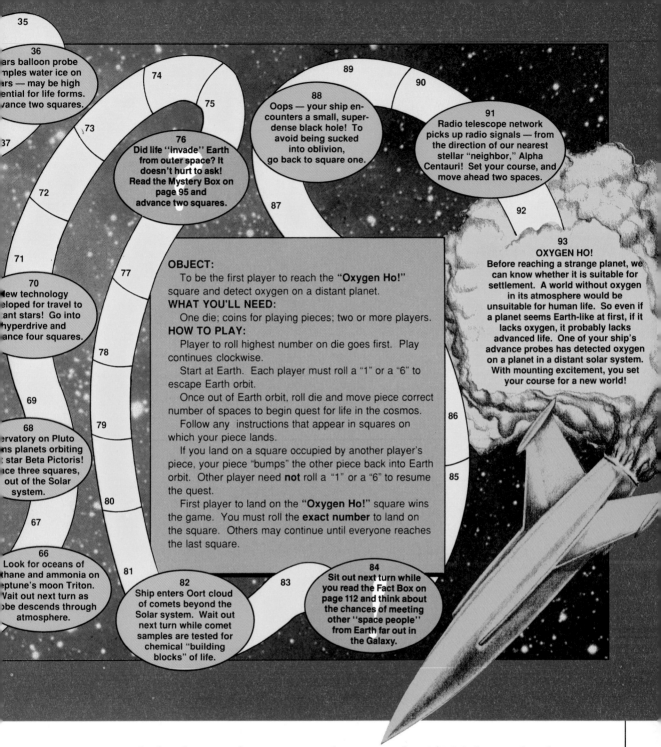

Mars, meanwhile, has a thin atmosphere, only 1/100th as thick as ours, and its surface is often colder than Antarctica! Jupiter is just a huge ball of mainly hydrogen, helium, and other gases, and so are the other large planets. Their moons seem to be lumps of rock and ice.

These are the facts as we know them. And we know from these facts that Earth is the only known planet that can support life like ours.

Can We Still Hope?

Though the other worlds of the Solar system can't support life like ours, might they have other, strange forms of life?

One of Jupiter's satellites, Europa, is covered with a worldwide glacier. Perhaps under the ice there is a large ocean. Might there be life forms in it that are completely different from anything on Earth?

One of Saturn's satellites, Titan, has a thick atmosphere, and one of Neptune's satellites, Triton, might also have one. Under those atmospheres, there might be oceans of methane or ammonia. Could there be strange life there, too? Some day we might go to those worlds to find out.

An artist imagines life existing in an ocean under the icy surface of Europa, one of Jupiter's moons.

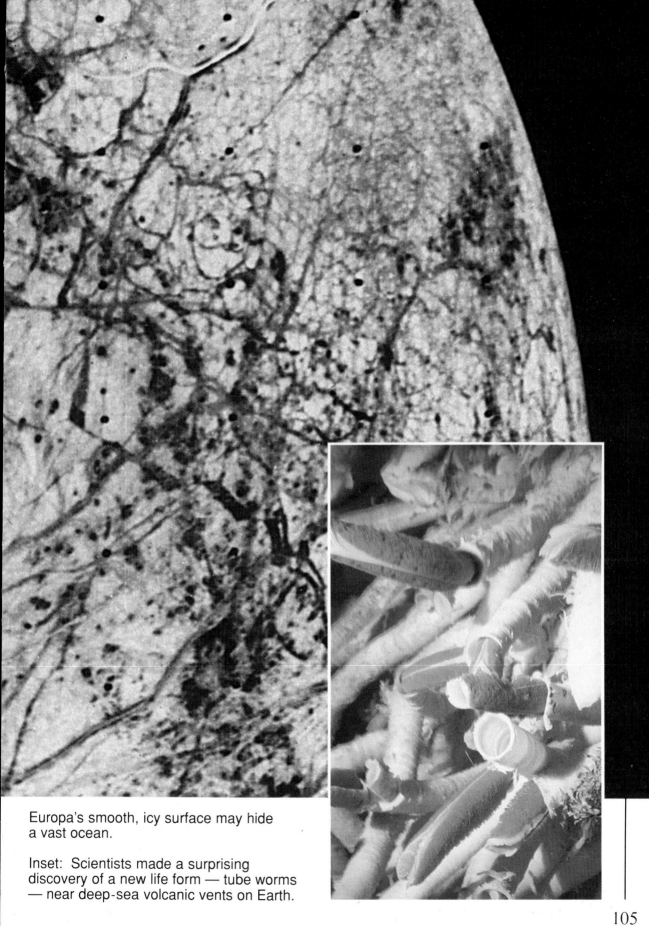

Europa's smooth, icy surface may hide
a vast ocean.

Inset: Scientists made a surprising
discovery of a new life form — tube worms
— near deep-sea volcanic vents on Earth.

The Universe Is a Big Place!

So we know there is no life like ours anywhere in the Solar system beyond Earth. And for now, we can only guess about the chances of even simpler life beyond Earth. But even if there is no life in the Solar system, there are other stars in our Galaxy and beyond, and many of them must have planets circling them.

Our Galaxy has about 200 billion stars, and there may be as many as 100 billion other galaxies. Even if only <u>one</u> <u>percent</u> of the stars are like our Sun, and only <u>one</u> <u>percent</u> of those stars have planets like Earth, that would still mean billions of billions of Earth-like planets. Perhaps on every one of them there is life, and on a few of them civilizations may have developed. Some may even be advanced far beyond ours. We have no way of telling so far. We can only speculate.

Opposite and below: We live on one of nine known planets orbiting our Sun (below) — one of 200 billion stars in the Milky Way (inset), which is but one of billions of other galaxies!

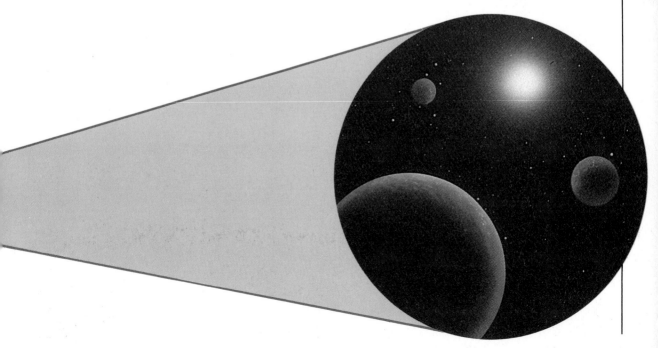

"What Would Life Be Like . . . ?"

Would life on some distant Earth-like planet seem familiar to us? Would there be creatures who look like human beings? Surely not! Even here on Earth, life takes a wide variety of shapes. Compare a whale and a crow; a praying mantis and a shark; a bacterium and an oak tree.

On other worlds, life would develop in strange ways to fit strange environments. Some might seem unpleasant to us, and some beautiful, but all of these possible life forms should be interesting.

Perhaps, in studying completely different life forms, we will understand all of life — and ourselves — better.

Looking for life in a harsh environment. Below: Lake Hoare on the frozen continent of Antarctica. Scientists are studying Antarctic lakes to get an idea about past environments on Mars.

Inset, opposite: The black, white, and green stripes are actually plant life called lichen (LIE-ken) growing in Antarctic sandstone.
Opposite: These rod-shaped bacteria grow along with the Antarctic lichen.

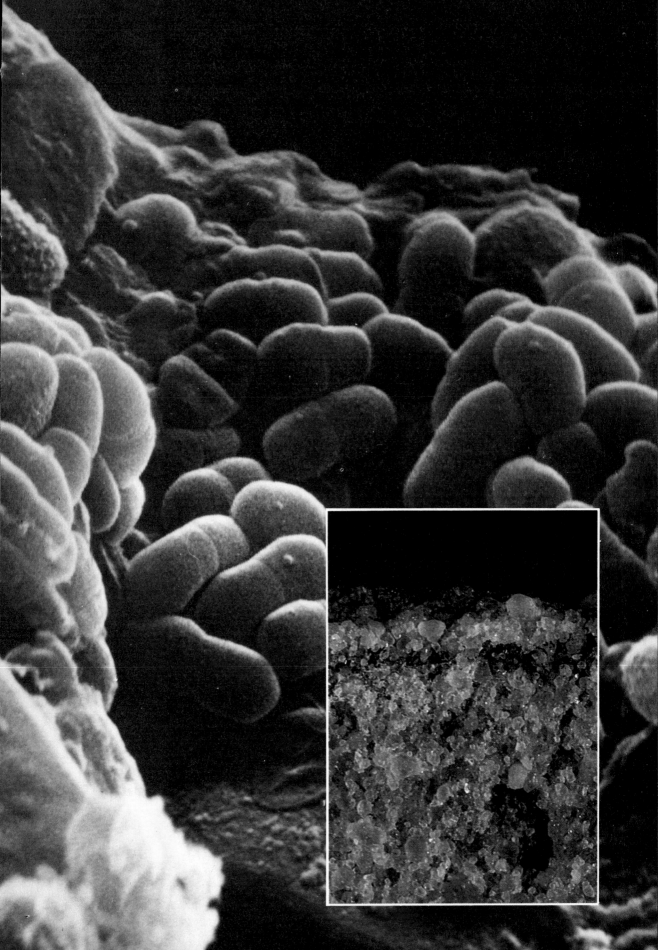

Are We Alone?

Suppose there is life on planets orbiting other stars. Can you imagine traveling to those planets to study those life forms? Rockets that take only a few days to reach the Moon, and a few months to reach Mars, would take many years to reach the stars.

Future rockets might travel 40,000 miles (64,000 km) each second, but they would still take more than 20 years to reach the nearest star. Even if you traveled at the speed of light (the fastest possible), it would take 100,000 years to go from one end of the Galaxy to another.

So even if there is advanced life out there among the stars, how will we reach it? Will we remain alone on our little planet?

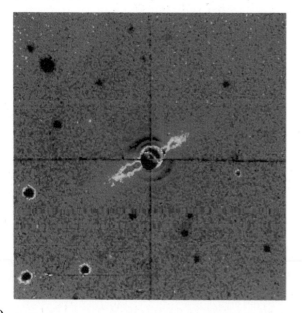

A disk of dust and gas encircles the star Beta Pictoris. In this photo, the disk is colored red and yellow; the star itself is masked out. Scientists believe the dust and gas are condensing into planets, forming a young solar system around the star.

Inset, opposite: Farewell to Earth. An interstellar spaceship leaves Earth orbit and begins its long voyage to the stars.

Opposite: The starship from Earth surveys its new home — the planetary system of a remote star.

The Universe-wide Civilization

Reaching the stars is not something we can do in a few weeks, months, or even years. But suppose we take our time. Suppose we build huge starships that are small worlds in themselves with 100,000 people aboard each one, and that these ships travel through space on voyages that take thousands of years. One ship might eventually reach one distant planet, while others would reach other planets.

Slowly, humanity would settle among the stars and perhaps encounter other forms of life. Of course, it would be difficult for one settlement to communicate with another, and each would develop in isolation. Earth would become a distant memory, and some day it might be forgotten altogether.

Our descendants might become "extraterrestrials" to other interstellar civilizations. And should their paths ever cross in the vastness of the cosmos, our spacefaring settlers might even become extraterrestrials to each other!

The distant galaxies — plenty to go around

There is room in our Galaxy for millions of settlements, each about a different star. Beyond our Galaxy, there are others. There are three small galaxies, the Magellanic Clouds, some 150,000 light-years away. The nearest large galaxy, larger than our own, is the Andromeda Galaxy, which is 2,200,000 light-years away. The farthest known galaxies may be 17 billion light-years away. We will never use up the Universe or see all its glories up close.

After centuries of travel, an Earth ship and its inhabitants prepare for arrival at a new world.

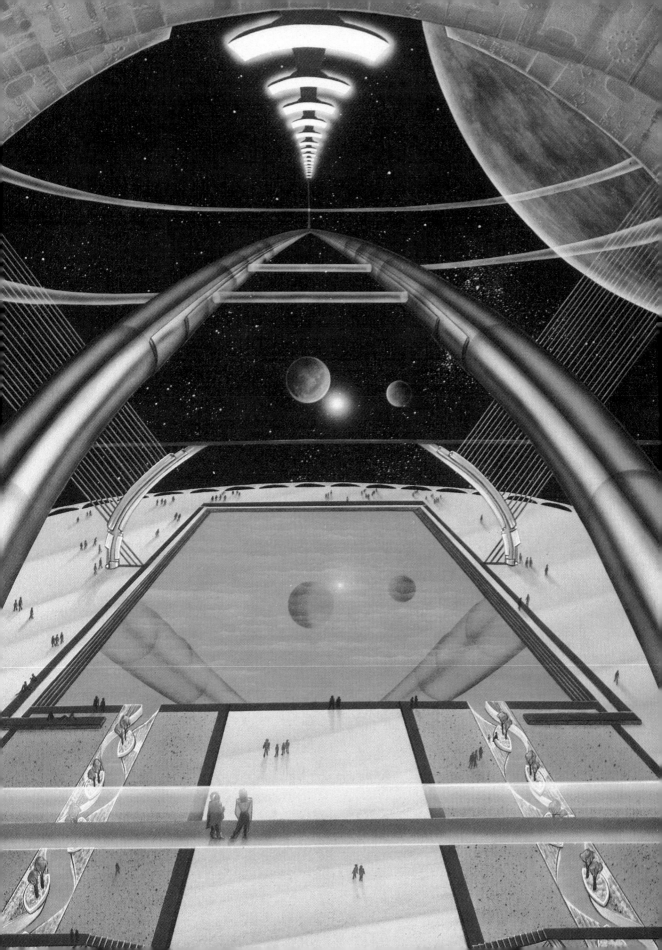

Facts about the Universe aren't always about the faraway. Right here on Earth, there were once giant animals called dinosaurs. About 65 million years ago, they disappeared. The reason why they vanished might be found in outer space. Out there we may discover not only the secret of the dinosaurs' end, but also fantastic dangers that could threaten our Earth in the future, and threaten us as well.

And it may be that by learning about space, we will be able to escape those dangers. *Isaac Asimov*

Did Comets Kill the Dinosaurs?

If people had lived in Montana when Tyrannosaurus did, he could have swallowed them whole.

Rudolf Zallinger/Peabody

Giants of the Earth

Once, millions of years ago, large animals called dinosaurs walked on Earth. Some of them were up to 90 feet (27.4 m) long. Others may have weighed as much as 100 tons or more — equal to about 12 large elephants!

The largest dinosaurs were plant-eaters, but the picture you see here is of a meat-eater, the most terrifying that ever lived. It is a tyrannosaur. It was nearly 50 feet (15.2 m) long and was heavier than most elephants. Its head was up to 5 feet (1.5 m) long, and its teeth could be over 7 inches (17.8 cm) long. It was not something you would want to meet!

Were some dinosaurs warm-blooded?

The dinosaurs were reptiles. We can tell that from the structure of their bones. All the reptiles that are alive now — turtles, lizards, snakes, alligators — are cold-blooded. This means that when the weather is cold, they're cold, too, and become very sluggish and slow in their movements. Some scientists are sure that some dinosaurs were quite active. These scientists wonder whether some of the dinosaurs were warm-blooded. After all, birds and mammals are descended from reptiles, and they are warm-blooded. When did that start? So far, there is no way to tell.

The Mystery of the Dinosaurs

The dinosaurs first evolved about 225 million years ago. For 140 million years, they ruled the Earth. Some kinds died out, but others came into being. Then, around 65 million years ago, they <u>all</u> died out. All we have left, now, are bones, teeth, footprints, and other fossils, or evidence of prehistoric life.

Why did dinosaurs die? Scientists have wondered if the climate changed, if small animals took to eating dinosaur eggs, or if a nearby exploding star showered Earth with deadly x-rays. No explanation seemed quite right.

© Diane Gabriel/Milwaukee Public Museum

The size and depth of a footprint can help scientists know how much a dinosaur weighed.

Not all fossils are underfoot. These fossils are in the wall, once underground, of a quarry in Colorado.

Ultraheavy . . . ultralong . . . ultratall: it's Ultrasaurus!

The largest known land animal of all time was a dinosaur called Ultrasaurus. The few bones discovered so far tell scientists that the animal must have weighed 100-140 tons and measured 100-115 feet (30-35 m) long and about 56 feet (17 m) tall — about three times as tall as a giraffe. This means it would have been as tall as a five-story house.

Death from Space?

In 1978, scientists found some rare materials called iridium in rocks that were about 65 million years old. There was more iridium in these rocks than in others, and it came just when the dinosaurs died. Where did it come from? Possibly from outer space. Meteoroids are rocks that move through space and sometimes collide with Earth. We often see them enter Earth's atmosphere as fiery meteors. Meteoroids that strike Earth's surface are called meteorites. Some meteorites are quite large. In Arizona there is a hole, or crater, gouged out by a large meteorite. Some craters are so old they've worn away, but scientists can detect signs of those craters from the air.

The Barringer Meteor Crater in Arizona is about 3/4 mile (1.2 km) across. Scientists think it was created by a meteorite impact 50,000 years ago. © Allan E. Morton

e of the world's most beautiful craters is in western Australia. It is called the
lf Creek Crater.

Global Winter

Could something striking Earth 65 million years ago have killed the dinosaurs? It could be so. If the object was big enough, it could have gouged out a huge quantity of rock and soil, ground it into dust, and flung that dust high in the air for miles and miles.

The dust would have spread out all over Earth. It would have blocked the sunlight. Little light or heat would have reached Earth for months, or even years. The plants would have died, and then large animals that ate plants or other animals would have died. Smaller animals might have nibbled at bark or seeds, or eaten the frozen bodies of larger animals. Some of them would have survived. But the dinosaurs would be gone.

Global winter: With dust blocking the Sun's heat and light, Earth would be cold and dark. Most plants and animals would die.

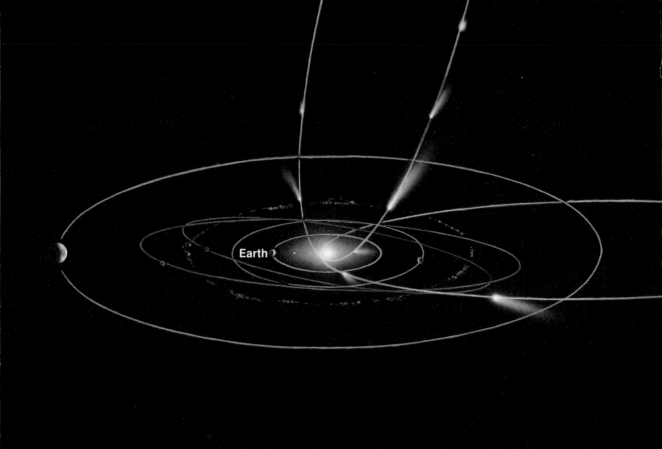

Earth-crossers: Some comets and asteroids travel dangerously close to Earth. In this picture, the paths of the comets are shown in yellow, and the paths of stray asteroids are in red.

Earth Under Fire

Are there large objects in space that can hit Earth? Yes. Scientists have detected objects a mile (1.6 km) or more across that can come within a few million miles of Earth. A couple of dozen of these have been detected, but there are probably others we just haven't seen. There may be more than a thousand in all. None of them comes close enough to hit us. But the gravitational pull of planets can change their paths.

Some day, one of these objects, on a changed path, might crash into us — just as one might have crashed into Earth 65 million years ago!

© Julian Baum (series of four)

© Mark Paternostro

Lured by Earth's gravitational pull, a meteoroid approaches our prehistoric world (1) and enters the atmosphere as a fiery meteor (2). Now a meteorite, it collides with Earth (3) as a dinosaur watches (4). Will this mean the end of his food supply?

Asteroid or Comet?

Some of these nearby objects are made of rock or metal. We call these objects asteroids. Others are made up mostly of ice, and we call these comets. If a comet were to hit Earth, it would speed through the air and heat up. The ice would vaporize to gas and expand in a loud explosion. It might not reach the ground and leave a crater, but it would do much damage.

An icy comet vaporizes as it speeds toward Earth. Its target: Siberia.

© Mark Paternostro

ГОРА „ОБЕДЕННАЯ". ВИД НА СЕВЕРО-ВОСТОК.

Сплошной ориентированный бурелом в 10-15 км от центральной площади.

...beria, site of a possible comet strike in 1908 near the Tunguska River. Leonid Kulik, ...Soviet scientist, investigated the blast in 1927. He described the area in this picture, ...ated February 24, 1929. The words are written in Russian, as you can see.

In 1908, something struck the middle of Siberia. It knocked down every tree in an area more than 11 miles (18 km) across. But it didn't kill anyone, because no one was living there. Some scientists believe the object was a small comet that exploded in the atmosphere before it could hit Earth.

Comets are made of lighter material than asteroids are. But if a comet is large enough, it can do as much damage as any asteroid.

The object that may have hit 65 million years ago didn't seem to leave a crater, so scientists thought it might have been a comet.

Of course, the object might have hit the ocean, and the crater might be at the bottom of the sea! In 1987, a huge crater was found in the sea bottom near Nova Scotia. It is 28 miles (45 km) across, and perhaps it is what is left of a possible collision that may have killed the dinosaurs.

Comets — a sign of doom?

In older times, before people knew what comets are, they thought comets were warnings from the heavens telling of upcoming disaster. When comets appeared in the sky, people were terrified. And sure enough, whenever a comet appeared something terrible would happen. A war would come, a plague would rage, or the king would die, or something. Of course, even when a comet <u>didn't</u> appear terrible things like that also happened. Somehow people never seemed to notice that.

The Nova Scotia crater as it might look deep beneath the sea: Could this be all that remains of what killed the dinosaurs?

Where Do Comets Come From?

If a comet is large enough, it might survive being heated by the air and gouge out a crater on land or under the sea. Some scientists think it was a comet, not an asteroid, that killed the dinosaurs. A Dutch astronomer, Jan Oort, believed that there are many billions of comets slowly orbiting the Sun many times farther away than the planets. This "Oort cloud" might be where Earth-colliders start from.

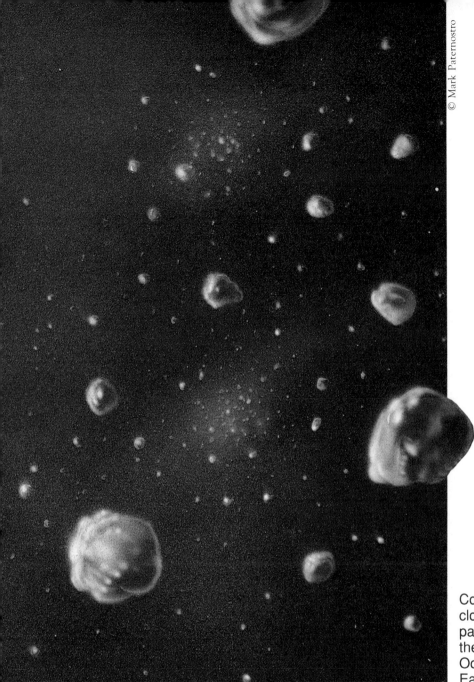

© Mark Paternostro

Comets in the Oort cloud: The gravity of passing stars may pull these comets out of the Oort cloud and into Earth's orbit.

Comets — a look back in time?

The Sun and the planets probably formed out of an original cloud of dust and gas. We can't be sure what the original cloud was made of. In the billions of years the Solar system has existed, the Sun and the planets have changed a lot. On Earth, for instance, some of the original matter was lost to space, and some sank to the center. Scientists think comets are samples of the original cloud that have <u>not</u> changed with the years. That is one reason they were so excited when spacecraft passed near Halley's Comet in 1986. It was the first time a comet was studied up close. Further studies on comets may tell us more about the beginnings of the Earth.

What Makes Showers?

Some scientists think that every 26 million years comets from the Oort cloud hit the Earth and cause different kinds of life forms to die out. It isn't hard to imagine a large comet striking Earth accidentally. But what could cause collisions to occur like clockwork every 26 million years?

One thought is that perhaps the Sun has a small, dark companion star that circles it once every 26 million years. This star has been named "Nemesis." At one end of its path, this little companion could enter the Oort cloud. Its gravitational pull would send billions of comets into our part of the Solar system. Some of those comets could hit Earth.

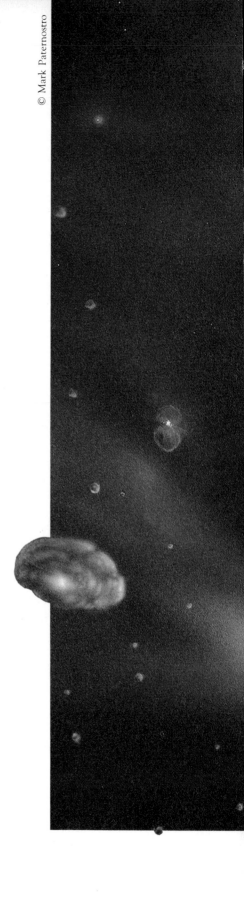

Nemesis: Does the Sun's companion
star come around every 26 million
years and cause trouble?

Orbiting the Galaxy

Nemesis is not the only possible explanation for regular collisions between Earth and comets. After all, Nemesis has never been seen, and we don't know for sure if it even exists. But we do know that the Sun travels about the center of our Galaxy, carrying Earth and all the planets and comets with it.

The Sombrero Galaxy: a star's wavy course across the galactic midline. Our Sun follows a wavy course that takes it above and below the galactic midline of the Milky Way, crossing the plane roughly every 33 million years.

The Sun follows a slightly wavy path, first above the midline of the Galaxy, then below it, then above it again, and so on. Every time it passes through the midline, where there are more stars and dust clouds, a stronger gravitational pull may send the comets into our neighborhood.

An Unknown Planet?

The Sun's passing through our Galaxy's midline may not explain these collisions, either. Some astronomers think the cause may be a distant planet we haven't detected yet. Perhaps when this planet is at the far end of its path around the Sun, it reaches the inner edge of the Oort cloud.

It would reach the far end of its path every few thousand years, but the orbit might wobble so that the far end would be above the Oort cloud or below it most of the time. Every 26 million years it would go through the cloud and send comets flying in our direction.

Planet X: Does a still unknown planet of the Solar system bump into the Oort cloud every 26 million years and send comets and asteroids to Earth? If so, such a planet would be so distant and faint that it would be hard to detect.

© Michael Carroll

Welcome back, stranger!

Sometimes, we may think a kind of animal is no longer alive, but then it surprises us. There is a fish called a "coelacanth" which was supposed to have died out along with the dinosaurs 65 million years ago. In 1938, a ship near South Africa caught a fish in its net that turned out to be a coelacanth. Since then over a dozen coelacanths have been caught. The coelacanth did not die out, but it lives in deep water and usually stays out of human sight.

Are there dinosaurs among us today?

Mammals are descended from certain early reptiles that were <u>not</u> dinosaurs. But birds may be descended from reptiles that <u>were</u> dinosaurs. Some scientists think that birds are still much like little dinosaurs that have grown feathers and become warm-blooded. So is it fair to say that dinosaurs have all vanished? Might we say that some of them sit in trees and sing? Scientists haven't made up their minds.

What's in Store for Earth?

We're about halfway between major comet strikes, if the theory of collisions every 26 million years is correct. We might be hit at any time, of course. But the real danger may not come for another 13 million years.

Will that be the end of human beings? Maybe not. By that time, we should have colonies on various bodies of the Solar system and we should have built cities in space.

We could be watching for the approach of any dangerous body. We could push it aside, or even destroy it, by using advanced science. Then we'd be sure that no collision from outer space could kill us the way it killed the dinosaurs.

If the comets are coming in just 13 million years, maybe we should plan to be out when they arrive. NASA scientists and engineers have designed permanent colonies. These colonies could be on other planets, such as Mars, or in space itself. This one looks like a giant wheel in space. A large mirror directs sunlight into the colony.

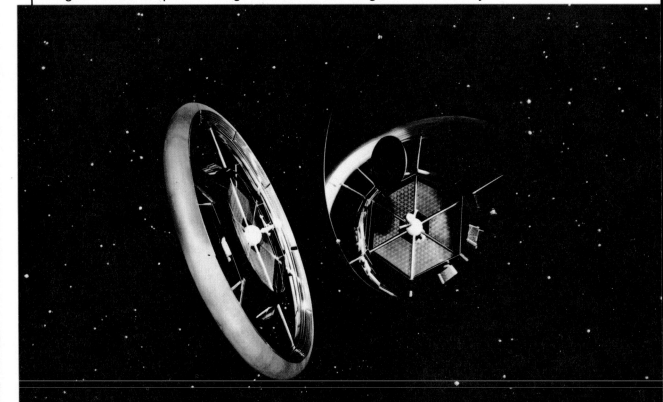

Space colony: home for 10,000 people 250,000 miles (402,000 km) from Earth. This space colony would be constructed of ore mined from the Moon.

This proposed space colony has a bridge like the Golden Gate Bridge in San Francisco. The colony would be a cylinder 19 miles (30.6 km) long and 4 miles (6.4 km) in diameter. In this picture, city lights are reflected in the large mirrored panels that direct sunlight into the colony.

Fact Files

How Was the Universe Born?

The Earth's Moon

Quasars, Pulsars, and Black Holes

Is There Life on Other Planets?

Did Comets Kill the Dinosaurs?

Fact File: Distance and Size in the Universe

We know the Universe is a big place. But just how big is it?

We can talk about the great distances and sizes that exist in the Universe. But maybe the best way to get an idea about just how big those distances and sizes really are is to compare them to distances and sizes we know about and use here on Earth.

Imagine that we could reduce the cosmos to a size we can manage. First let's imagine that we could make the Sun the size of a soccer ball. Then let's shrink the Universe even further, so we could put the entire Solar system in a coffee cup. And finally, let's shrink the entire known Universe down so that all of our Galaxy, the Milky Way, would be no wider than a long-playing record!

Even after reducing the Universe this much, we might be surprised at how far apart everything in the cosmos still seems. We can use the illustration above and the charts on page 143 to get an idea of how big and how far everything is out there—and how much space there is in space.

The Sun as a Soccer Ball

What if the Sun was...	Then Earth (our home planet) could be...	And Jupiter (the Solar system's biggest planet) would be...	And Pluto (our Solar system's tiniest known planet) could be...	And Alpha Centauri (the nearest star in our Galaxy) would be...
...a soccer ball about 8 3/4 inches (22 cm) wide?	...a pebble less than 1/10 inch (1/4 cm) wide, and about 78 1/2 feet (24 m) from our soccer-ball Sun.	...a bit bigger than a ball bearing 7/8 inch (2.2 cm) wide.	...a pebble tinier even than Earth, and over 1/2 mile (0.8 km) from our soccer-ball Sun.	...nearly 4 miles (6.4 km) from the soccer-ball Sun at the center of our Solar system.

The Solar System in a Cup

And what if our Solar system was...	Then the Milky Way (our Galaxy) would be...
...small enough to fit in a coffee cup?	...as wide as North America — about 3,000 miles (4,800 km) across!

The Milky Way as a Long-playing Record!

And what if the Milky Way (our Galaxy) was...	Then the Andromeda Galaxy (the galaxy "next door") would be...	And the farthest-known quasars would be...
...a long-playing record about 1 foot (30 cm) wide?	...23 feet (7 m) away from the Milky Way.	...more than 32 miles (51 km) away from the Milky Way!

As big as we think Earth is, it is only a tiny speck in our vast Universe!

Fact File: The Moon's Craters

Today, thanks to Lunar probes and piloted missions, we have seen the Moon's craters close up, as well as something never before seen by humans — the far side, which always faces <u>away</u> from Earth. On these two pages, you can examine two interesting questions about the Moon's craters: 1) How were they formed? 2) Why are the craters on the far side so different from the ones on the near side?

How Were the Moon's Craters Formed?

By the Impact of Meteorites	By Volcanic Action

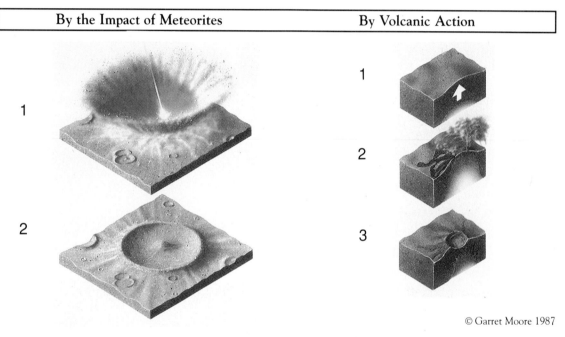

© Garret Moore 1987

1. Meteorite strikes the Moon's surface, sending out a shock wave that gouges out deep hole, and throwing up a cone-shaped curtain of boulders and other debris that fall back to surface.

2. The boulders create several smaller craters around the first one, and the finer debris settles into a blanket.

Comments:
• Upon impact meteorite is consumed, or absorbed, into its crater.
• Matter at center of impact "rebounds," just as a drop in a pool of water would, and freezes.
• Thin lines, or filaments, emerge as blanket of dust settles. Pattern of lines called <u>rays</u> extends outward from crater.
• Most of Moon's craters have been formed by impact of meteorites.

1. Portion of surface forced upward by melted rock and gases from within Moon's interior.

2. Eruptions of gas and lava through Lunar surface and into sky above. Pressure from below now eased.

3. Collapse of surface into a crater.

Comments:
• Signs of volcanic crater differ from those of meteorite crater.
• No rays, smaller craters nearby, or "peak" at center of volcanic crater.
• Volcanic craters are a sign that Moon once had a very active, hot inner region.
• Unlikely there would be any current volcanic activity on Moon — just some possible shifting or adjusting of Moon's surface. These shifts might give rise to an occasional volcanic "burp" of trapped gas.

Comparing Craters — The Near Side vs. the Far Side

Lick Observatory

Near Side

As these photos illustrate, the Moon's near side has fewer craters of the type found on the far side. But it has more of the maria, or "seas," that show up as large dark areas. The maria are actually the result of volcanic activity that covered ancient meteorite-impact craters with flowing lava. Why did so much more volcanic activity occur on the near side, and why did so many more meteorites seem to have struck the far side? Scientists aren't sure.

Far Side

Perhaps more meteor strikes occurred on the far side because Earth partly "blocked" the near side from meteoroids. And, perhaps, there were more volcanic eruptions on the near side because of the pull of Earth's gravity on the gases and melted rock below the Moon's surface. No one knows for sure.

NASA

A

© Michael Carroll 1987

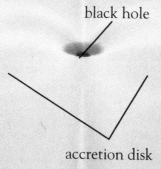

gas jet

black hole

accretion disk

B

Fact File: Quasars and Black Holes

Quasars. What we can see of them comes to us from distances so vast that we can barely imagine how far away — and how long ago — they existed. Some are believed to be 12 billion light-years away, and for years astronomers thought they were the oldest visible objects in the Universe. Astronomers now believe they have spotted objects that could be as distant as 17 billion light-years away. These are primeval galaxies. We see them as they were in the earliest stages of their creation, before the Universe was old enough to spawn quasars. But quasars still win the prize for power, since most astronomers still believe that they are the most powerful energy sources in the sky.

On the opposite page are two pictures. Picture A is of a spiral galaxy with a quasar at its core. Picture B gives us a close-up of the core, showing the black hole that may lie at the heart of a quasar.

Picture A:

Subject:
- A violent spiral galaxy deep in the cosmos.

Special features:
- High-energy quasar at galactic core.
- Possible black hole at center.
- Accretion disk — a gravitational whirlpool of hot gas in a ring around the center feeding the black hole and the quasar.
- Gas jets spewing excess particles at right angles to disk.

Picture B:

Subject:
- A detailed view of the galactic core, showing the quasar and its black hole center.

Special features:
- Sideways view of accretion disk. The disk might stretch out to a diameter 100 times that of our Solar system.
- Black hole at center of disk. Because of huge amount of stellar matter swirling around the center, the black hole would not normally be visible. A black hole like this might have the mass of billions of stars the size of our Sun crammed into a space no bigger than that of our Solar system.
- Jets shooting matter at a right angle to the accretion disk. This is matter that is in excess of what the black hole can absorb. The matter shoots out to distances that could approach millions of light-years. This would be farther than the distance between our Milky Way and its nearest galactic neighbor, the Andromeda galaxy.

Fact File: Looking for Life in "Uninhabited" Places

So far, we haven't found any life on other planets. But does this mean that other planets are uninhabited? If we haven't found any life in a specific place, such as a distant planet or even a house down the street, we might call that place "uninhabited." But we might be amazed to discover how an "uninhabited" house actually teems with life forms — even if we don't see any of these life forms at first glance. Many of these forms seem alien to us, and they live under conditions that might seem hostile to life. The photographs and numbered chart on these two pages show just a few of these life forms.

Could it be that, like our "uninhabited" house, other planets harbor unusual life forms surviving under harsh conditions — and that we just haven't found them yet?

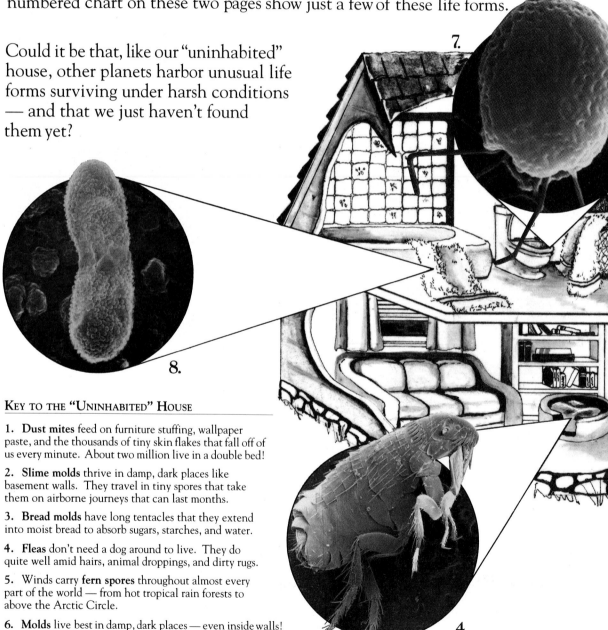

KEY TO THE "UNINHABITED" HOUSE

1. Dust mites feed on furniture stuffing, wallpaper paste, and the thousands of tiny skin flakes that fall off of us every minute. About two million live in a double bed!

2. Slime molds thrive in damp, dark places like basement walls. They travel in tiny spores that take them on airborne journeys that can last months.

3. Bread molds have long tentacles that they extend into moist bread to absorb sugars, starches, and water.

4. Fleas don't need a dog around to live. They do quite well amid hairs, animal droppings, and dirty rugs.

5. Winds carry **fern spores** throughout almost every part of the world — from hot tropical rain forests to above the Arctic Circle.

6. Molds live best in damp, dark places — even inside walls!

7. Some **bacteria** exist in tough "houses" that protect them against hostile surroundings.

8. Some life forms need surroundings that would kill other life forms, including humans. For example, this **bacterium** needs an environment <u>without</u> air!

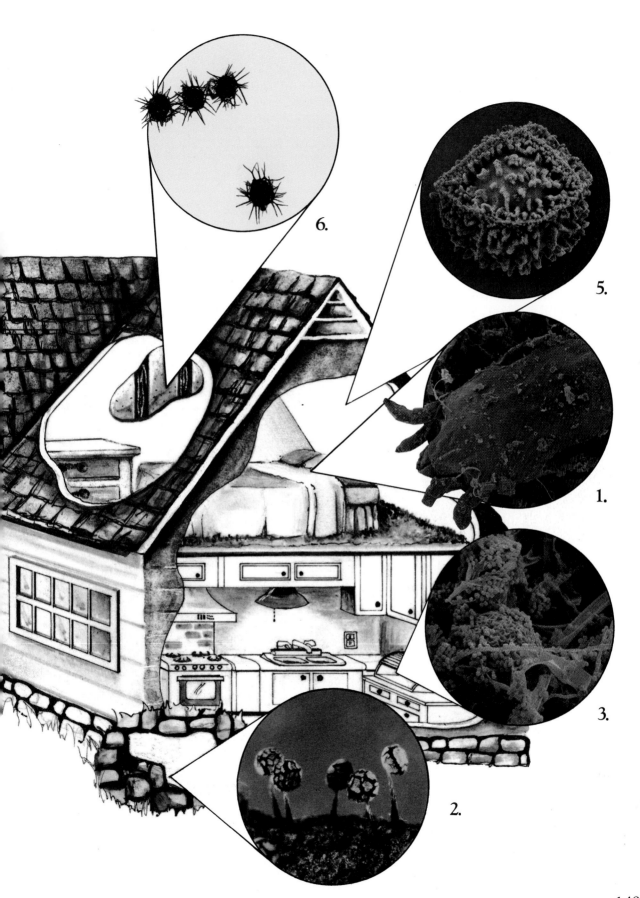

6.

5.

1.

2.

3.

Fact File: Did Comets Kill the Dinosaurs?

Why Did the Dinosaurs and Other Prehistoric Reptiles Die Out?

POSSIBLE CAUSES	POSSIBLE EFFECTS
Changes in climate	Some types of plants disappeared, leaving some dinosaurs without food
Small animals eating dinosaur eggs	Fewer dinosaurs reaching adulthood and reproducing
Major catastrophes or natural disruptions on Earth - such as the rise of mountain chains, huge floods, or volcanic eruptions	Sudden death of plant and animal life

The Age of Reptiles

Here is a pictorial walk back through prehistory. Our walk begins at the left, with the time 65 million years ago. This is when dinosaurs disappeared from the face of the Earth. Our walk ends at the far right, some 400 million years ago, before the Age of Reptiles began. Dots above the names will help you find the animals in the picture.

CRETACEOUS PERIOD   JURASSIC PERIOD

65   135
Millions of Years Ago

Triceratops   Pteranodon   Anatosaurus   Rhamphorhynchus   Allosa
                                                                                    Stegosaurus
Triceratops   Tyrannosaurus   Apatosaurus (Brontosaurus)
                                                                      Archaeopteryx
150   Ankylosaurus   Archaeopt

Why Did the Dinosaurs and Other Prehistoric Reptiles Die Out?

POSSIBLE CAUSES	POSSIBLE EFFECTS
An asteroid or a very large meteorite striking the Earth	Dust thrown out from the impact blocking out light and heat from the Sun for months or years, killing plants and causing large animals that ate plants to die, too
Comet strike or shower	Life-forms die out, kinds and numbers depending on how much damage done by comet
A nearby star exploding	Earth showered with deadly X-rays

Rudolf Zallinger/Peabody

TRIASSIC PERIOD	PERMIAN PERIOD	CARBONIFEROUS PERIOD	DEVONIAN PERIOD

190   225   280   345   400
Millions of Years Ago

Plateosaurus
Sphenacodon
ptosaurus
Dimetrodon
Eryops
Podokesaurus
Limnoscelis
Diplovertebron
Cynognathus
Edaphosaurus
Ophiacodon
Eogyrinus
Seymouria
psognathus
Saltoposuchus
Varanosaurus
Meganeuron

151

Glossary _____

Andromeda Galaxy: the closest spiral galaxy to our own, although it is over 2,000,000 light-years away.

Armstrong, Neil: the first person to touch the Moon's surface (1969).

asteroids: objects in space made of rock or metal that orbit the Sun between Mars and Jupiter. An asteroid can be from one to several hundred miles (km) in diameter.

astronauts: men and women who travel in space.

atmosphere: the gases that surround a planet, star, or moon.

atoms: the smallest particles of elements that can exist. They are the source of nuclear energy when joined together or split apart.

bacteria: the smallest and simplest forms of cell life. A bacterium is one-celled and can live in soil, water, air, food, plants, and animals, including humans.

Bell, Jocelyn: the astronomer who first detected what later were known as pulsars.

the Big Bang: a gigantic explosion that some scientists believe created the Universe.

billion: in North America—and in this book— the number represented by 1 followed by nine zeroes—1,000,000,000. In some places, such as the United Kingdom (Britain), this number called "a thousand million."

black hole: an object in space caused by the explosion and collapse of a star. This object is so tightly packed that not even light can escape the force of its gravity.

canal: a river or waterway made by people to move water from one place to another. It was once thought that the narrow, dark markings on Mars were canals built by Martians to move water from the ice caps to the desert areas.

carbon dioxide: a heavy, colorless, odorless gas. Carbon dioxide is what gives soda its fizz, and when humans and other animals breathe out, they exhale carbon dioxide.

colony: a group of people settled in a place away from their original home.

comet: an object made of ice, rock and gas; it has a vapor tail that may be seen when the comet's orbit is close to the Sun.

Copernicus, Nicolaus: the first modern scholar to suggest, in 1543, that the Sun was at the center of the Universe, with the planets orbiting around it.

Crab Nebula: a huge expanding cloud of dust and gas that is visible from Earth. It was first reported in 1054 and is the result of a supernova.

crater: a hole in the ground caused by the impact of a meteorite striking Earth.

decade: a period of 10 years.

Doppler, Christian: the Austrian scientist who, in 1842, showed why noise sounds more shrill when coming toward you, but sounds deeper when moving away from you. Light waves act in a similar way. They are shorter—and appear blue —when they are coming toward you, and become longer—and appear red—when moving away. (See also *red shift*.)

eclipse: when one body crosses through the shadow of another. During a Solar eclipse (eclipse of the Sun), parts of the Earth are in the shadow of the Moon as the Moon cuts right across the Sun and hides it for a period of time.

eclipse of the Moon (Lunar eclipse): what occurs when the Moon is full and on the opposite side of Earth from the Sun, and then passes through Earth's shadow.

eclipse of the Sun (Solar eclipse): when the Moon cuts right across the Sun and hides it for a while. An eclipse of the sun usually only lasts a few minutes.

evolve: to develop or change over a long period of time.

extraterrestrial: "outside of Earth." Extraterrestrial refers to forms of life that do not begin on Earth.

full Moon: what we call the Moon when it is on the opposite side of Earth from the Sun so that it is lit in its entirety.

galaxy: any of the billions of large groupings of stars, gas, and dust that exist in the Universe. Our Galaxy is known as the Milky Way Galaxy.

Galileo: an Italian scientist who made a telescope and got the first clear view of the Moon's surface.

glacier: an enormous layer of ice formed from compacted snow, often itself carrying a layer of snow.

gravity: the force that causes objects like the Earth and Moon to be attracted to one another.

Hawking, Stephen: a scientist who has shown that black holes can slowly evaporate and turn into thin gas.

helium: a light, colorless gas that makes up part of every star.

Herschel, William: the German astronomer who, in 1785, showed that the visible stars are all part of a vast collection of stars. He said that our Sun was part of this collection, which today we know as the *Milky Way Galaxy*.

hoax: an act that is intended to deceive.

host: a living organism on which or in which lives another organism, called a parasite.

hydrogen: a colorless, odorless gas that is the simplest and lightest of the elements. Stars are three-quarters hydrogen.

interstellar: between or among the stars.

iridium: a rare element that occurs more in extraterrestrial objects than in Earth's crust.

light-year: the distance that light travels in one year—nearly six trillion miles (9.6 trillion km).

Lunar Orbiters: vehicles that flew to the Moon and photographed all parts of it, including the previously unseen far side.

lunar years: the basis for ancient calendars. There would be 12 new Moons from one spring to the next.

mare: (pronounced "MAH-ray") the Latin word for "sea." The plural of "mare" is "maria" (pronounced "mah-REE-ah"). People once thought the Moon's flat dark areas contained water, and so they called these areas maria. Today we know they were caused by volcanic eruptions producing lava flows.

meteor: a meteoroid that has entered the Earth's atmosphere.

meteorite: what is left of a meteoroid once it hits Earth.

meteoroid: a lump of rock or metal drifting through space. Meteoroids can be as big as asteroids or as small as specks of dust.

methane: an odorless, colorless, flammable gas. It is an important source of hydrogen.

Milky Way: the name of our Galaxy.

Moon: Earth's only satellite. It is about 250,000 miles (400,000 km) from us.

nebula: a cloud of dust and gas in space. Some large nebulas, or nebulae, are the birthplaces of stars. Other nebulae are the debris of dying stars.

neutron star: a star with all the mass of an ordinary large star that has had its mass squeezed into a small ball.

Oort cloud: a Dutch astronomer, Jan Oort, believed that there are many billions of comets slowly orbiting the Sun many times farther away than the planets. This "Oort cloud" might be where Earth-colliders start from.

optical illusion: something perceived by the eye, a camera, or a telescope that is not what it appears to be. For example, the appearance of a "bridge" of gases from a quasar to a galaxy may be false, a trick played on the "eye" of the telescope—an optical illusion.

organism: anything that lives, such as a bacterium, a rose, a human—including any plant or animal.

Orion Nebula: one of the huge clouds of dust and gas in which stars are forming.

oxygen: the gas in Earth's atmosphere that makes human and animal life possible. Simple life forms changed carbon dioxide to oxygen as life evolved on Earth.

phases: the periods when the Moon is partly lit by the Sun. It takes about one month to progress from full Moon to full Moon.

Pluto-Charon: the combination of planet and moon that is the nearest thing to a double planet. Astronomers believe that Pluto and Charon may even share the same atmosphere.

probe: a craft that travels in space, photographing celestial bodies and even landing on some of them.

pulsar: a neutron star sending out rapid pulses of light or electrical waves.

quasar: a "star-like" core of a galaxy that may have a large black hole at its center,

radiation: the spreading of heat, light, or other forms of energy by rays or waves.

radio telescope: an instrument that uses a radio receiver and antenna to both see into space and listen for messages from space.

radio waves: electromagnetic waves that can be detected by radio receiving equipment.

red giants: huge stars that develop when their hydrogen runs low and the extra heat makes them expand. Their outer layers then change to a cool red.

red shift: the apparent reddening of light given off by an object moving away from us (see *Doppler*). The greater the red shift of light from a distant galaxy, the farther that galaxy is moving away from us.

satellite: a smaller body orbiting a larger body. The moon is Earth's *natural* satellite. Sputnik 1 and Sputnik 2 were Earth's first *artificial* satellites.

science fiction: fiction, or stories, in which actual, imagined, and sometimes possible future discoveries in science form part of the story.

"seas": the name for the flat dark areas on the Moon or Mars, even though they are completely waterless. Any one of these "seas" is actually called a "mare" (pronounced "MAH-ray").

SETI: "Search for Extraterrestrial Intelligence"; the search for signs of extraterrestrial intelligence by trying to detect any radio signals that such intelligence might use.

Solar system: the Sun with the planets and all other bodies that orbit the Sun.

speculate: to imagine or think deeply about something.

sphere: a globe-like body. The ancient Greeks believed that Earth was a large sphere at the center of the Universe.

spore: a single cell from which a new organism can grow.

sulfuric acid: a liquid that is capable of burning, wearing away, or dissolving many materials.

supernova: a red giant that has collapsed, heating its cool outer layers and causing explosions.

terraform: to make another world Earth-like by giving it qualities that are, as far as we know, special to Earth, such as an atmosphere and water. "Terra" is Latin for "earth."

Universe: everything that we know exists and believe may exist.

vaporize: to turn something that is liquid or solid into a gas.

variable stars: stars whose brightness changes. Some variable stars change brightness very regularly. Others are unpredictable.

white dwarf: the small, white-hot body that remains when a star like our Sun collapses.

x-rays: a form of radiation that has a shorter wavelength than visible light and can thus pass through materials such as flesh and bones. The shorter its wavelength, the more easily an x-ray passes through a material.

Index